Without a Mask

Without a Mask
Discovering Your Authentic Self

Avikal Costantino

BOOKS

Winchester, UK
Washington, USA

First published by O-Books, 2011
O-Books is an imprint of John Hunt Publishing Ltd., Laurel House, Station Approach,
Alresford, Hants, SO24 9JH, UK
office1@o-books.net
www.o-books.com

For distributor details and how to order please visit the 'Ordering' section on our website.

Text copyright: Avikal Costantino 2010

ISBN: 978-1-84694-533-5

A CIP catalogue record for this book is available from the British Library.

Design: David Kerby

Printed in the UK by CPI Antony Rowe
Printed in the USA by Offset Paperback Mfrs, Inc

We operate a distinctive and ethical publishing philosophy in all
areas of our business, from our global network of authors to
production and worldwide distribution.

CONTENTS

Contents

There are only two mistakes one can make along the road to truth: the first is not going all the way; and the second not starting.
Buddha

Every person born into this world represents something new, something that never existed before, something original and unique.
Martin Buber

PROLOGUE

I wouldn't know how to define what makes us human, for me there's no definition that's wide enough. What I do know – and perhaps you too – is that each one of us is hiding underneath layers and layers of pretension and that we can instead choose to peel away these layers and recognize what is hiding underneath. I also know that we can do our best to live an authentic life and involve ourselves in practical ways, day after day, taking the responsibility for being alive now, in this moment, in this place, with the totality of ourselves. Choosing to be alive and true to ourselves is not that easy because it means moving away from the pack and stepping out into unknown and unexplored territory. The territory is unknown because it is the present: new, fresh, never happened before, and it is here that life is happening. But, driven by survival instinct and fear of life itself, we are constantly drawn back to our past in a relentless search for answers and methods, while we look to the future with fear and apprehension. On the other hand, to be genuinely alive, now, means recognizing that our past is no more and the future has not yet arrived: only THIS present moment belongs to us. Therefore the necessary condition for being authentic is that I need to be present: to exist in the here and now, with my body, my emotions, my mind and spirit, and an alignment of all that existence has given me since the day I was born and makes me what I am: a unique human being.

The conditions essential for my presence are:
1. The ability to be fully conscious of my experience in the present moment.
2. A will that sustains my commitment and consciously frees me from all that conditions me and causes me to react in an automatic way to reality: a way that is repetitive, reactive, predetermined and unaware.

You don't need a particular philosophy or spirituality to realize that each moment is always new, that even when our minds tell us it has already happened, this is never true. Everything changes, continually. Life is just like Heraclites described it more than two millenniums ago; a river that flows continuously. Each time we dip our foot into the water, what we are touching is a completely new river. The river of existence never fails to provide an ever-changing pureness, one moment after the next. If we recognize this true reality and simply accept the evidence of its truth, then inevitably we'll end up asking ourselves how come life seems so often devoid of significance, repetitive, stressful, like a storm cloud of misfortune pelting down on us. A duty rather than a pleasure. A problem rather than a mystery. A sacrifice rather than an adventure. If this is what you believe and feel, and it leaves you ill or frustrated, without hope or just restless, then ask yourself; if life is an inexhaustible source of new opportunities, a constant current of transformation and possibility, how come you don't experience things this way? Where did you get lost? Where did you lay down the aliveness of this moment and allow your old, boring, bygone, predictable past crawl over and hide the present? Where were you when you stopped moving and why do you now cling on so tightly to this fixed and immovable thing? What do you gain from this? What is so petrifying about living?

Recognizing Obstacles
If you consciously accept that everything changes, what will become of your reality? : That the approaching moment is unknown and unpredictable and that the present moment is the only thing within your grasp and that you can rely on. The past has gone leaving just a memory, the future has not yet arrived and you are here in the present, and this present is the ground from which your future moments will take shape and those that follow, and so on. Then a new question arises: how to approach this moment/opportunity, how to enjoy it, how to live it as fully as possible? How can I be

myself? How can I understand and experience the significance of the life presented before me, here, while I am writing, while you are reading, while I am listening to the wind outside, while you are sensing the heat of your body or listening to the sounds around you, while you are watching the words slide across the page in front of your eyes? Who is reading? Who is aware of how their bodies feel? Who feels warm or cold? Who is thinking about what they're reading? Who is aware of their thoughts, words and sensations? Who, from a hidden corner in the soul, feels that there's more to existence than simply getting up in the morning, going to work, eating, sleeping, growing old and.... and then an enormous void ? Look. Feel. Ask yourself. Listen to what your heart is saying to you. What is your body telling you? Feel existence calling you back, YOU, NOW. If life didn't want you, you wouldn't be here. If the universe didn't want YOU, here/now, you wouldn't exist. You are UNIQUE in this moment, on this planet. Are you here? Have you arrived? Are you walking on this earth? Can you feel the air you are breathing, your body as it moves, the sounds around you and the warmth of your skin. Are you here? Are you here, now? Have you touched ground? Are your feet in contact with this planet and its gravity? Are you PRESENT?

The endeavor of this book is to deal with the main obstacles that prevent our presence, in a way that will enable you to consciously remove these obstacles while offering you the necessary techniques in order to accomplish this, because one thing is clear: *you can live totally in the here and now only if YOU are totally present. And only by being fully present can you also discover who you really are, beyond the name you carry, the conditioning you have received, the color of your skin, the religion you follow, the work you do and the country in which you live.*

This book is a call to your soul, a song for your heart and an invitation to your passion.

Inquiry, meditations and visualizations

In the following chapters you will find sections called "inquiry" or "meditations" or "visualizations" where I propose themes for exploring issues related to that chapter, particular meditation or visualization techniques. Inquiry is not just analysis, and neither is it limited to the field of logical deduction. On the contrary, inquiry brings us face to face with the unknown, challenging everything that we think and understand. An inquiry is dynamic and living, and if approached with inquisitiveness and passion, will take us outside our "zone of comfort and survival," unlocking territories well beyond our expectations and guiding us towards and into profound and instant understandings that would be impossible using linear logic.

Inquiry is made up of five fundamental steps:

1. Set out a question for your exploration that gives you a general direction of where you want to go.

2. Tell the "story" and go through what you already know about the subject matter.

3. Widen your attention and note how this commentary influences your present: the sensations in your body, your emotions, images and thoughts as they appear in your consciousness.

4. Observe whether there is automatic judgment, whether in relation to what you are saying or the way you approach the inquiry.

5. Don't be in a rush to reach conclusions. Be curious and continue to ask questions about your topic, your reactions now, your understanding of what is happening. Why are you experiencing certain symptoms and how they relate to the emotions you are feeling and what lies behind particular underlying tensions. Keep exploring, following the thread while it gradually unravels, even if the meaning seems obscure or fragmented. Let understanding come by itself.

PART 1

PERSONALITY:

PRISON AND PROTECTION

CHAPTER I

THE GREAT BETRAYAL

"The present cannot be recognized by the ego, because it is always covered by the past".
A.H.Almaas

Sometimes we realize that we are not 'real'. Sparked off by an unexpected crisis, from something we read in the eyes of a close friend, a gap in mid sentence or in the unfocusing of our eyes as we turn our attention within, this sudden bolt of awareness arrives with a powerful blow and leaves us limp with vague feelings of guilt and long-rooted shame. And a sadness; a familiar sadness that we feel even if we have rejected it or forgotten about it. A sadness that is a memory made of images in the mind, of feelings in our heart and sensations in the depths of our stomach. A memory of a true self, spontaneous, unguarded, open and genuine. Normally this sadness is soon swept up and swathed in a cloak of fear: the fear that others will realize we are fake and fear of the consequences of ever trying to be our real selves again.

When did you stop being yourself?

Perhaps you don't remember, perhaps you do. Most people I have met, and those I have worked with, often don't actually remember that moment when they stepped outside, closing the door behind them and with it, their true selves. It may take days, months or even years of searching, trawling over past events, memories of a childhood in which we felt so alien and detached from our families and the environment in which we lived: So different from the people around us, from our brothers or our sisters, and above all, from our mothers and fathers. We relive those painful sensations of not belonging, those lost and frightening feelings, not knowing which way to turn for comfort and support. We remember how we felt alone, isolated, different. Sometimes we also remember how angry we felt, insulted and violated by what the world wanted from us; to disown ourselves, to forget our true nature, to hide from our hearts, to disband the spontaneity of being ourselves, and then give in, abandoning ourselves, becoming just like them – the adults – just as they wanted. The great betrayal is that moment in which every child is forced to leave behind his true identity, to forget what the Zen masters called "the Original Face", and to disguise himself in the fancy outfits of personality, don the mask of survival and pretension. This phase in a child's development arrives, painfully and inevitably. There is no escape, there is nowhere to run, there are no half measures, the demands are completely clear: if you want to be accepted, recognized and loved, if you want to be part of our world, you have to renounce yourself, you have to conform, adapt, be led and accept that we adults know what you need, better than you. If you want to be part of your family, your society, your race, your country, the religion into which you were born, you have to take yourself to pieces and sacrifice your wholeness. You must reject your sexuality as it is sinful and "dirty". You must curb your intelligence and, instead, listen to those with experience and who know best. You must rein in your natural intuition and heed the truths that they teach you, even if none of them practice what they preach. Learn to doubt your desires, your vitality, your spontaneity. Take heed when they tell you that you are too much: too noisy, too aggressive, too excitable, too wild, too lively. Adapt yourself, tone down, rein in, shield, barricade, shut the beast away. And above all FORGET.

The great betrayal is the culmination of a long, drawn out process of separation from our true nature and of adapting to existing ways and values, morals and ethics of the environment in which we live. The great betrayal brings us to a standstill, crystallizing the growth of the child into a hard, almost impenetrable structure of survival; this is the personality, carefully sculptured from imposed standards and rules. At about the age of seven or eight, the child is forced to become a slave to the past and to renounce the unpredictability of a spontaneous and natural growth. The fluidity of his natural awareness; his ready, spontaneous embrace of the present moment is squeezed and crushed into a rigid framework built from pre-packaged information, a framework whose purpose is to defend us from the inevitable unpredictability of the present and to teach us to react in an automatic way based on past experiences as imparted by the adults. The efficiency of the individual's repression and adjustment to collective norms is guaranteed by the internalization of his familiar authority figures, both familial (mother and father first of all) and social (teachers, religious figures etc). These figures of authority glue together and culminate in the formation of the inner judge or superego[1]; the psychosomatic structure in charge of maintaining the status quo of the personality and inhibit transformation.

How did we arrive at the great betrayal?

Every parent has the responsibility to provide their children with the necessary tools to make their way through daily life and so an essential part of a child's growth and education is the sharing of their parents' knowledge and experience. This includes their moral values, their beliefs, experience of relationships, their self-perception and that of the world, religious doctrines, political and social beliefs, and so on. This transmission is a sort of "programming" of the infant through which he becomes capable of evaluating, regulating and controlling his own organism and the way it relates to the external world. To operate efficiently this "programming" has to introduce categories such as good and bad, acceptable and non-acceptable, beautiful and ugly, right and wrong, which means a vision of the inner and external realities based on separation, dualism, opposite poles and conflict. The inner reality of a child is divided into light and darkness: In the light are all the behaviors and values upheld by his parents and other key figures of authority from his childhood and in the shadow are all those condemned as unacceptable. The natural predisposition of the organism toward survival, the need for parental love and acceptance, fear of rejection and punishment, push the child inevitably towards adapting to the imprinted "programming" or, by another name, obedience to "environmental conditioning". This process of conditioning is reinforced by school and society at large. The pressure to adapt and obey are fundamental aspects in the formation of a child's self-identity, whether internally or externally, with regard to the social environment in which he lives and, above all, with his family. In order for the conditioning to be effective, the rules of survival, as laid down by the coercive external agencies (parents), must be internalized at infancy. This is effected through the formation of the superego (the inner judge), the psychosomatic presence that, through judgments, prejudices, opinions, admonishments, guilt, shame and other forms of punishment, becomes the inner agency that controls and directs our every action and behavior, assigning value and significance to the existence of the individual. Around the age of seven or eight the process of creating the personality is usually finalized with the formation of a stable inner judge, a fixed set of values to be withheld and an even greater set of values that it considers unacceptable and are henceforth banished to the unconscious.

Adapting to survive

It is in this final phase that a sort of internal pressure forces each individual towards a fundamental choice: belong to us (family, society etc.) or be alone, exiled, isolated. The price is the sacrifice of our individuality, the prize is to belong to the community in which we live and the promise of survival within, and thanks to, this community. This pressure demands absolute identification with the social mask (personality); the approved instrument of survival of the community in which we live. The personality is like the clothes we wear; clothing that protects us and helps others and ourselves to identify who we are: every time I get dressed I have an immediate sense of identity, a special personal history, a social belonging. I know who I am because I have specific values, particular opinions and a certain way of looking at the world. I know who I am because I experience things in a certain way and I have a certain way of speaking and specific likes and dislikes. I know who I am because I have a particular set of emotions that are familiar to me and a network of physical tensions which I am accustomed to. I know who I am because my body has a particular shape and because I view myself in a certain way. I know who I am because I believe that there are things in me that are acceptable and presentable, and things which are totally unacceptable that must remain hidden. I know who I am because I have memories of the past and the sense of a thread that keeps these memories together. I know who I am because I have a recognized position in a particular family, social circle, religion, race. I know who I am because I am a teacher, a doctor, an office worker, a carpenter, a secretary. I have one or more social roles that help define who I am.

Why do I need a personality?

The personality is like a suit that we put on every morning as soon as we get up. This familiar clothing, easily picked out, worn habitually, is what makes me feel like me. It is made from all the tensions I carry around with me, internal noises and density, temperature, the movements I make and positions I adopt, of repeated perceptions, of repeated thought patterns, repeated judgments, repeated emotions, repeated beliefs and repeated opinions about me and about reality. The personality - that which I believe myself to be - is an item of clothing that maybe somewhat threadbare and boring, but it is also comfortable and reassuring.

The personality therefore performs several basic functions:

1. It offers me limited and easily established ground from which I

identify myself one moment after another, enabling me to maintain a sense of identity that is more or less stable.

2. It offers me pre-arranged interpretations of the reality around me; values, opinions, judgments, moral categories and ethics. Its instruments enable me to make my way through the world and survive.

3. It enables me to interact with the world, establishing the relationship between that which I consider to be Me (the content of the shell of my skin) and everything else (not Me).

4. It gives me a fundamental sense of certainty based on my past and on believing I know who I am, what is me and how I fit in relation to reality and how the world fits around me.

But is this really true? Do I really know who I am? Do I really know what is real and what is not? What is right and what is wrong and how to function in this world guided by these criteria? Am I really confident in myself and in the world? Am I really walking my path with certainty and trust? Generally, the initial response is yes. To put under scrutiny the real nature of our personality, our sense of personal identity and our vision of the world is a revolutionary act that can stir up deep fear and memories of painful childhood events. To doubt the status quo and its apparent consistency is an act of rebellion against our inner judge (and everything that it has taught us) that might spark off negative repercussions and punishments not so different from those we experienced as children when we refused to adhere to family authority and scholastic rules. To say no to our superego, or simply doubt the necessity of an internal control system leads to self-punishment through guilt, shame, depression, isolation, lack of energy, confusion, impotence and vulnerability. It is very rare that we are taught to think with our heads, feel with our hearts and act from our guts. It is very rare that we are taught to believe in ourselves, to follow our natural intuition and use our natural capacity to respond spontaneously. The main, inner core round which the structure of the personality continues to aggregate is, in most cases, profoundly conservative and basically paranoid: It follows the old routes in order to avoid risks and change. It maintains a fixed sense of identity therefore defending its opinions and points of view. It doesn't trust anyone, the world is hostile and dangerous. It doesn't get too close to anyone, life is already a struggle so avoid confrontation. It doesn't move too much, stay still so that no-one can see or recognize you, if you stand out you will be attacked.... and so on.

Therefore we can regard the personality also as an attempt to hide, from ourselves and others, a basic internal conflict between the need to know ourselves in a direct, immediate and spontaneous way, and the need for safety, belonging and protection.

Unfortunately it seems that almost every human being is convinced that spontaneity and control, the unforeseen and safety, self-truth and social acceptance are incompatible elements. In most cases, the great betrayal carried out in infancy continues to push us towards social adjustment and to abandon our true selves. But what would happen if we stopped betraying ourselves? What would happen if we began to deliberately take the mask to pieces, to uncover our original face? What would happen if we began to venture into the discovery of our uniqueness and potentiality?

"...the real world is the world of Being, the world of the Now. One must see from the perspective of Being to have an idea of how far away from reality the perception of ego actually is. It comes as a shock to those who have this privilege...Seeing reality without the filter of the past is a cataclysmic experience, which uncovers forces and energies which are not even conceived by the ego". [2]

Inquiry

In this part of the chapter I would like to propose some themes to explore that will help you to deepen your understanding of what you have just read and above all, to make it personal. The issues to explore are keys with which you can "unlock" your unconscious, revisit your personal past and get to know yourself in a more intimate way. You can do this exploration alone (better written) or with someone who is close to you and interested, who like you, is undergoing this inner journey. The exploration not only helps to activate and bring to consciousness things that aren't normally at the front of your mind, but also to metabolize things you have avoided because, in the past, they were considered unacceptable, things to avoid, or hide. This exploration opens up rich territories of potentiality, passions and desires and helps you to expand your old usual boundaries, unearthing new capacities along the way.

Explore the questions that follow. Take at least fifteen minutes for each one and repeat the exploration after a few weeks.

1. Have you ever felt you are not really real, alive? Have you ever felt like you are living behind a mask? You feel like you are hiding your true self from others (and maybe even yourself)? What do you remember about those occasions when this happened, what were the circumstances? Where did it happen, how, when? Were you alone or in company? Can you remember the emotions you felt at the time? How are you feeling right now as you relive those situations? What physical sensations are you feeling? What emotions do these memories bring? Is there an automatic process of self-judgment present as you explore? And if there is, what judgments are you aware of?

2. Have you ever felt completely real, completely alive? What do you remember about those experiences? Make a list, as detailed as possible, of the physical sensations, your emotions, feelings, understanding and revelations from those events. It may help to close your eyes and visualize the situation: the place, the atmosphere, the position of your body, what was happening inside you and around you, your sense of time.

3. What relationship do you have with your personality? Are you satisfied with how you are, or not? What do you like about yourself and what would you like to change? If you had to rate your self-acceptance on a scale of one to ten, what would your score be? If you

had to rate your self-satisfaction what would your score be? If you had to rate your ability to be sincere with yourself and others, what would your score be?

4. What do you feel when the people around you cast doubts (whether openly or not) on your sincerity, honesty, openness? How do you react? Are you offended, angry, do you shrink back, do you feel misunderstood, or maybe something else?

5. What was the family atmosphere like when you were an adolescent? Did you feel supported when you were trying to work out who you were? Were there opportunities to talk and discuss things? Were you allowed to make mistakes? Were you encouraged to say what you thought? Did you feel understood and encouraged to be yourself? What sensations and emotions come up as you remember these things?

Visualization

Sit down comfortably and close your eyes. Concentrate on how your body is feeling, without trying to exert control over what you are feeling, instead, let your attention wander but stay focused on the body. If you find that you get distracted by something, just go back to concentrating on your body. After a few minutes begin to visualize yourself when you were an adolescent: bring back the images of that time; your family environment and note what kind of emotions are associated with those images, what kind of physical sensations you feel while remembering. Ask yourself: how did I feel about family life then? Let your thoughts flow freely. After a few minutes, try to go further back in time, to when you were seven or eight. Remember the house where you lived, your bedroom, the mealtime atmosphere, how you felt when you looked at your parents. Once again, concentrate on the physical sensations and emotions these memories arouse. Take care not to start judging yourself or your memories. Use your will to let go of these judgments and stay present with the images that are emerging. Don't force yourself to understand or "adjust" your feelings. Don't change anything, simply look, listen and feel. Be an observer: just watch, leave everything as it is.

[1] I deal in detail with the Inner Judge in my book "Freedom to be yourself. Mastering the Inner Judge", IBI publications, Sydney 2007
[2] Almaas A.H., The Pearl Beyond Price, pages 55,56

CHAPTER II

SELF-IMAGE AND THE IMAGE OF OUR WORLD

"Your heart is crying and weeping but you keep smiling. You try to hold on to your image. You cannot be natural, you cannot allow your heart, your body, your mind to function in a natural way. You keep manipulating them. You choose: what can be expressed and what must be repressed. That repressed part becomes your unconscious"
Osho

Central to the personality is the sense of oneself, the sense of existing and of having one's own personal identity. Normally, we take it for granted that this sense of oneself and the perception of being an individual (separate from the world in which we live) have been with us since birth. The reality is quite different.

The sense of Self is not born with us
In "The Psychological Birth of the Human Infant: Symbiosis and Individuation", Margaret Mahler illustrates in great detail how the sense of self is formed through a process that begins around the fourth month of a child's development and carries on for the first three years of life, becoming the center of what we call self-identity. This sense of self is formed by the child in relation to the world around him but, above all, in relation to the people who have particular significance in his life: mother, father, brothers and sisters, grandparents. Day by day, the baby begins to perceive himself as being an entity in his own right, quite separate from those things which he now perceives as external objects: his mother's breast, her body, the cot, his own body etc.

During this phase, known as separation-individuation, the baby begins to gain experience of himself through the progress of separation from the mother, physically, mentally and emotionally. He emerges from the symbiotic union with his mother, characteristic of the first few months of life, and begins to discover his own inner world, initiating separation and self-government. As a result of this distancing, he begins to formulate mental boundaries that differentiate between internal and external, himself from another, the "here" and "there". The process of individuation is the baby's discovery that he exists as an individual, separate from the mother, able to maneuver himself and perceive, with the capacity to interact with other objects and make use of his own body in an independent way. It is a discovery of autonomy at every level that generates enormous resources and opens up incredible potentiality in the baby who, at the same time, is going through profound and contradictory emotional and physical circumstances. These circumstances relate to the uncertainty of the child with respect to his own resources and the awareness of his own strength, his need for external support on the one hand and his capacity for self-support on the other, his desire for fusion with his mother and the adventure of discovering himself and an unknown world, the need for reflection and acceptance from the mother and the sense of his own intrinsic value. The infant see-saws continually between two extremes: on the one hand he is gaining experience as an individual, realizing his own capacity, above all on a physical level, and enjoying the independence that his new mobility offers him. On the other hand he discovers limitations, the fear of separation, frustration, insecurity and impotence. The process of separation/individuation involves issues that accompany us for the rest of our lives: in our inner world, in our relationships and, more generally, the relationship we have with existence itself and the world in which we live.

Sense of identity and self-image

It is in the first three years of life that a sense of identity, separate from the mother, but in relation to her, is formed. For that branch of modern psychology known as "Object relation theory", the sense of one's own identity exists as a collection of memories based on mental representations. The infant begins to progressively remember himself (that is his own image of himself) and the mother (his image of her) during their interaction. As times passes memories accumulate and become systemized, fusing together to form a complete picture which remains essentially consistent over time. All the images related to himself form a complete image of the Self, those of the mother a complete image of her, those of other people, and so on. This final image of Self is what we call personal identity or the egoic identity.

Almaas summarizes this concept in the following words:

"The achievement of a separate individuality depends on two conditions:

The establishment of a cohesive self-image. *In fact, the sense of being an individual is nothing but taking oneself to be this self-image. In other words, the individual is a mental structure, a construct in the mind. Before this construct is developed, according to object relation theory, there is no sense of being a person.*

The internalization of a positively regarded image of the mother (the "good mother"). *The individual, that is the self-image, is supported psychically by the presence of the mother's image; thus the child does not feel alone when physically separate from the mother. He feels supported by the presence of the mother's image, which gives him the sense of security which allows him to be away from her and makes it safer to regard her as an autonomous person".*

"...the sense of being an individual is not only a developmental achievement, but is a feeling that results from identifying with a certain structure in the mind, the self-image. That is, to take oneself to be a person, separate from others, with one's own volition, is simply to identify with this construct in the mind".[3]

We identify ourselves with limitations.

The self-image is constituted of hundreds of boundaries that define and set the limits of an individual's experience. For example, if my self image is that of someone who is timid and incapable, this image will present itself in a particular way through my body, my emotions, my thoughts, it will affect how I express myself, the way I feel when I have to present my work, how I get on with the opposite sex, how I drive and dress, what I believe my opportunities to be, my sense of enjoyment, and so on. Identifying with an inner image of "timidity" implies breathing timidly, laughing timidly, moving and speaking timidly... the image of timidness becomes a psychosomatic boundary that I can never ignore and to which I must adapt or struggle against. Every boundary becomes a limitation and a battle zone inside which my inner dialogues and the dynamics with my inner judge play out. These self-boundaries, the products of childhood conditioning, even determine our thoughts: what is acceptable to think is determined by my personal history and my sense of identity, and the more we are aware of our inner programming the more we will realize that what we think and how we feel doesn't happen by chance. Everything is, in fact, determined by the sphere of what is acceptable or not acceptable to think and feel, based on our personal upbringing, the environment in which we grew up and collective values. The good news is that the more aware we are of the boundaries of our self-image the more they tend to loosen up: the personality structure, under the light of exploration and the intensity of our curiosity, begins to lose its rigidity, unfreeze. For example, I might discover that while it may be true that there are situations in which I feel timid and incapable, there are also others in which I feel confident and self assured. Perhaps I can begin to take some risks, accept that I might make mistakes and learn from these mistakes. At that point maybe I will think back to my childhood home; to how we weren't allowed to make mistakes and how humiliating it was to be found out and reprehended. Bringing back past events into consciousness can help liberate blocked energy and help us to understand our present behaviors, discarding old opinions and outmoded images. It is like peeling an onion, throwing away the outer layers and shedding light on those that are fresh and crisp. As psychic boundaries associated with different components of our self-image begin to fall away we become aware of a great spaciousness; the sensation of having more room to maneuver; physically, mentally and emotionally. You breathe better, you feel less oppressed, constricted, tied down. The natural spaciousness of Being presents itself as a lightness and freshness and also as curiosity: who would I really be if I wasn't always timid? Who am I really if I can make mistakes? Who am I if I don't have to continually stick to the rigidity of my images? Who am I if my system purifies itself; gets rid of the old and opens itself up to the present and the new?

Understanding the implications of the psychic structuring that happened in infancy is the key to understanding where the sense of unreality, precariousness, and inconsistency that we experience when we identify ourselves with the personality mask come from. Images formed by the memory and held together by our personal history have taken the place of immediate and direct (not manipulated) perception of ourselves and the things around us. The memory and its images of love have taken, and continue to take, the place of love itself, the memory and its anticipation of enjoyment take the place of enjoyment itself, memories of the other take the place of the other in the present moment.

Memories and images are veils that hide the direct experience of what is now. The direct experience of who I am at this moment is independent of memories, concepts, definitions, images or whatever structures that deal with the past and future: who I am is who I am NOW, and to be able to experience my nature it is indispensable that I free myself from the veils which hide it.

"Human beings are born into the realm of Being, and from the beginning manifest the true differentiated aspects of Being. This Being is never totally lost, and actually manifests in the child in predictable and supportable ways. It is true that the awareness of this Being is lost in the process of the structuring of and identification with the ego, but by understanding in detail this structuring, and the patterns of identification, we can actually remember in detail the process of our "forgetting". We can remember,

understand and undo this forgetting, retrieving what has been suppressed and opening the way for growing into true maturity and realization".[4]

Inquiry

1. Explore: what is your ideal self-image? How would you like to be? Make a list, as detailed as possible, of the qualities you have and would like to have. In what way is this image connected, positively or negatively, to your past and to your family. To the education you underwent and the values that were passed on to you. Feel what happens in your body as your mind explores. Observe whether you are under attack by your inner judge. What type of emotions do you feel?

2. Now explore your social image. How do you present yourself to the world and how do you feel about it? What image do you want others to see? What are the essential traits of this image? Do you feel like you live up to the image you portray, or not? Has your image ever collapsed? And, if the answer is yes, in what circumstances and with what effects? Do you feel you have to make an effort to maintain this image? In what ways do you make an effort? Be precise: situations, people, and particular aspects of your life. Note what's happening in your body as you explore. In particular, note if there are any tensions and where. And whether there is a sense of relief and liberation.

3. Now explore your inner image: how do you perceive yourself from the inside and how is this image different from that which you present to the world? How do you avoid feeling the inconsistency between these two images? Where are the conflicts? How do you deal with these conflicts? What effects do they have on your daily life?

4. Explore your image from the point of view of self-value: there is a positive image to which we are attached and that we want to show, and a negative image (to which we are also attached) that we tend to hide. What is the positive image and what is the negative? What are the "acceptable" qualities that make up the positive image and what

are the "unacceptable" qualities that make up the negative image? How do you hide your "dark side"? What happens if it emerges? Do you remember times in your childhood when certain things about you were chastised and punished? What were they? Is there a correlation between those events and your negative image?

5. How do you see your body? How should it be? What is the external image of your body and what is the internal image? What emotions do you feel while you are going through this exploration? Do memories come to mind of your childhood, if yes, which?

Visualization

Sit down or lie down on your back and make yourself comfortable. Uncross your legs and lay your hands on your lap without them touching each other. Breathe slowly, calmly and effortlessly. Let your shoulders relax. Open up your consciousness to the images, the sensations and memories of the past. Think about your parents and let their images appear, note how you see them, the atmosphere, what emotions you feel, their look, whether you hear their voices, how warm or cold you feel inside and out. Take one parent at a time and explore your images: as you see them. What are the fundamental ingredients of these images? Feel, listen, look and note what happens to you when you look at these inner images of your parents. Don't change anything, simply observe.

[3] Almaas A,H., The Pearl Beyond Price, p.25
[4] ibidem, p.31

PART II
FREEDOM AND
RESPONSIBILITY

CHAPTER III

REMEMBER YOURSELF

What makes the present so different? Obviously, my presence. I am real for I am always now, in the present, and what is with me now shares my reality. The past is memory, the future – in imagination.
Nisargadatta Maharaji

Our personal history is not really our past but just a particular interpretation of past events. An interpretation with which we identify ourselves completely and through which we justify, reinforce and recreate our sense of identity. This interpretation, fixed in time and repeated to ourselves and to countless others, becomes TRUE and RIGHT. We are honestly convinced that our lives happened in the way that we remember and recount to others. We believe in our history, even when we realize that other people, who have shared this same part of life, remember it in a different way. To recognize that my personal history is not the Truth with a capital T, but only a personal interpretation, a relatively limited truth and defined from my point of view, is not so easy.

In my own personal history, up until some years ago, I had two pillars that shaped the inner image of myself and all my perceptions of the world. The first was my identification with having been a victim of my brother: bigger than me, stronger than me and more impulsive. The image of myself was founded on a fundamental belief of having been persecuted and humiliated by him during a great part of my childhood. This firm conviction had not only selectively cancelled all of another part of the reality, but had also become the justification for a central element of my personality: anger and the desire for revenge. On becoming adult I found myself searching the world for reasons to fight, wrongs to right, maltreatment to revenge, challenges in which I could prove to myself that I was strong.....

for sure, stronger than him (my brother). Of course, all this came about in an unconscious, but compulsive way, I was aggressive and provocative and I didn't even realize it. I was running away from my sense of inferiority, trying to prove my invulnerability.

The second pillar was a conviction that my mother had always loved him more than me (yes, him again, my elder brother...). In adulthood, the effect was substantial uncertainty of my worthiness of being loved, hidden behind a stance of arrogant aloofness. The "dark, handsome man" was the external image of an internal package made up of the fear of intimacy, anxiety and uncontrollable emotions. At the same time this image enabled me to maintain a "safe" distance from others and a "necessary" emotional control.

Naturally, my personal history and the whole of the structure of my personality was revolving around and was based on these two (and other) fundamental beliefs and established an image of myself as the "solitary warrior" or, if you prefer, the archetypal hero. This image was my mission, my protection, my armor.

Up until the time I began to question this stronghold, everything was more or less okay. Every now and then I had some doubts as to whether things had gone as I wanted to believe, but it was easier to keep things as they were. My mask was safe. I WAS SAFE and nobody could hurt me behind this mask. Of course, no-one could really get close either but, in reality, it was a price I was willing to pay in the name of survival. My armor was heavy and the warrior could never really put down his shield. Isolation was a wound in my heart and a craving in my stomach. I was completely exhausted from the effort of keeping this image of myself upright and, if I remember correctly, I was thirty-three years old. It was then that I began to take a good look inside and to want to see the truth and begin to REMEMBER.

Recalling is remembrance

An understanding that all the great mystical and spiritual traditions share is that of the fundamental need to "remember oneself".

Moreover, they maintain that "remembering yourself" is an essential and inevitable part of the spiritual path. Remembering yourself means, little by little, abandoning your idea of existing as an ego, a separate "I" locked up in a physical body, controlled by overwhelming waves of emotions and the tyranny of mind, a slave to time and limitations, and acknowledge your soul and spiritual nature: the authentic self, the point of light, the primary energy, the original face, the being part of God.

Remembering yourself is a process of remembrance that has three fundamental aspects:

1. Bringing back to consciousness, repressed materials that have been banished to the unconscious; removed memories, events we have cancelled and denied. Repression and denial have left enormous holes in our psyche that manifest themselves in discontinuity in the perception of ourselves, empty spaces that we avoid for fear of pain and punishment.
2. Literally speaking, remembering also means re-member and that is, to put together again. Reunite, reconnect, reunify the parts of our physical body and, even more so, those of our spirit.
3. Remembering ourselves is, above all, the conscious shift of attention to Self, to the subject of experience itself rather than on the objects we experience.

For most people the sense of ego-identity which lies at the center of the personality is a fragmented experience, discontinuous, without solidity and substance. It is a vague sense of being, but one that comes and goes, like in a mist where things appear and disappear depending on the circumstances. For many, the experience of existing is almost completely dependent on being seen, recognized, and approved of by others (and by our own inner judge). **A clear and stable sense of Self is missing.** Re-membering is a conscious process in which we unify the parts: physical body, emotional body, mind and soul. It is also a reunion of the senses: seeing, listening and feeling INSIDE ourselves, not only outside.

The glue that holds us together.

The glue that tries to keep our personality together and give it a sense of integrity and substance is what is known as our "personal history" and, more precisely, our attachment to that history. Our personal history is like the sound track in a film where the action changes, events unfold, there is tragedy and comedy, pain, passion, success and failure, relationships and abandonment, adventure and ruin and everything is emphasized, supported and enclosed in the particular details of our personal history. It is the main thread that seems to make up cohesive episodes; memories, opinions, habits, emotions and frames of thought, physical sensations that I recognize as MINE because they appear in a certain way, they have a certain taste, underline and reinforce my identity. My personal history is, exactly MINE, it is about ME and it defines me.

And in my personal history there are some main threads that characterize the plot. Of course, the essential thing is me, the leading actor in the story, and then, inevitably, there are others: mother, father, brothers and sisters (if you have any), aunties and uncles, wives, husbands, sons and daughters, friends, enemies, teachers, pets, lovers and love rivals, colleagues etc. The list is certainly long, but if you look hard you'll find there are very few really important actors: many appear but few take center stage. As well as other human beings, you may also note that there are some particular ways of feeling, of behaving, specific ways of seeing yourself and the world that keep appearing in the same way or reappear with slight variations in time. For example you might note your tendency to live your daily life with the need to intellectually understand what is happening, or that it is only in your heart where you find the capacity to live with what happens, or that an instinctive drive and a particular sensation in your stomach are guiding your life. You might realize that your first automatic reaction is fear and the need to hide, or the uncertainty of how others see you and the need for approval, or anger and the need to control. You might recognize a sense of separation and lack of intimacy with your body or vice versa, a faith in your intelligence or the conviction of not being so smart, the need to help or of being right at all cost, and so on.

Personal history is the ensemble of the images of your self, of the key people with whom you are (or were) in a relationship with and the image of the world that you have, plus the affective qualities that characterize your relationships between you and other people, whether that "other" is your mother, your brother, your first love or the office boss, the house in which you live, the job that you do or your life in general.

While the structure of the personality is sometimes a little difficult to contemplate, understand or feel in a personal way, our history is continuously with us, we live inside it, we tell it to ourselves and others, we know its smell and its taste and we see its lights and shadows. While the personality seems to be something psychologists and therapists make a living through, our personal history is our home, familiar and predictable.

We pay a lot of attention to it and it is also quite easy to recognize the attachment we have to our history.

The movement of attachment

As we have seen in the previous chapters, the sense of our identity is a collection of images of me, of others and of reality in general. My attachment is what sustains and recreates these images and, more precisely, the incredible speed and almost imperceptible movement with which I separate myself from the present moment and attach myself to an image from the past that exists in my memory. This movement of removal from the present is incredibly fast, habitual and essentially unconscious. My attention literally shifts from direct experience of the present moment and attaches itself to a past image that contains sensorial, conceptual and emotional aspects. This shift produces certain results:

1. The present is covered by a mantle of the past: an interpretation and comment on what is here/now (including myself) through what I have already experienced.

2. Frozen mental representations deny and obscure the dynamic freshness of reality.

3. I protect myself from change and I create an illusion of control, shifting my attention from the unpredictability of the events in their present form to familiar mental categories and I convince myself that I can control the future.

4. I move my awareness of feeling/attention from my stomach and from my heart to thinking/imagination in my head.

5. The movement through which I attach myself to the past, because of its speed, creates the illusion of a continuity of my personal history.

On this subject Don Juan, a Yaqui sorcerer and Carlo Castaneda's teacher, explaining the importance of becoming conscious of how the inner dialogue creates the personal history and how this sustains a rigid and dead description of the world, says:

"We talk to ourselves incessantly about our world. In fact we maintain our world with our internal talk. And whenever we finish talking to ourselves about ourselves and our world, the world is always as it should be. We renew it, we rekindle it with life, we uphold it with our internal talk. Not only that, but we also choose our paths as we talk to ourselves. Thus we repeat the same choices over and over until the day we die, because we keep on repeating the same internal talk over and over until the day we die".[5]

Dissolving the attachment to personal history

Through our past interactions with the world we have accumulated millions of bits of information that are stored in our energetic fields whether they serve us or not. An important, if not fundamental, part in the recovery of our integrity and discovery of our uniqueness is our liberation from these past images that no longer fit our present: images of ourselves that are obsolete, infantile, limited, that hold us back, interfering with our capacity to grow and the expression of our potentiality.

In an instinctive way, unorganized and fundamentally unconsciously, I began to sum up my life when I was about twenty-seven years old at the end of a long period of political and social militancy, as the radical dreams of the political movement of 1968 started collapsing. A profound longing to be myself and a passionate curiosity regarding the purpose of my life guided me without me realizing. It was then that I began my recapitulation (that is still ongoing).

Recapitulating our own personal history means opening ourselves up to the story that we tell, listening to ourselves and taking note of the empty spaces and the discontinuity. It means opening yourself up to those voids and recognizing the process of repression that generated them, allowing the memories and feelings to emerge. It means creating connections between happenings, events, phases of our development. It means examining yourself and waiting for the answers, the revelations, the unexpected winces of understanding that you didn't expect. It means putting things in order, taking things back on and integrating them.

Recapitulation is an act of love that points us towards the fundamental unity of the Self, and towards the union of the Self and the reality in which we live. In recapitulating I remember and in remembering I reconnect and in reconnecting I begin to experience myself as a whole, a harmony, and not a fragmented and confused being, not a separate being, full of shadows. It is the natural luminosity of my soul that reveals itself in remembering.

Recapitulation is also an exercise for discharging and then recharging the body with energy, recalling and revisiting one's own personal history. We free ourselves from suppositions, prejudices and preconceptions. It reactivates blocked energy in our organs, our nervous system, endocrine and muscular systems and restores harmony. Recapitulation is remembering, or rather, consciously reliving events and past experiences.

Recapitulating our personal history

Recapitulating is the method we use for recognizing and dissolving our attachment to our personal history. Practicing recapitulation helps you to:

1. Clean out useless past images and unburden yourself from a lot of weight that you are carrying around..

2. Make your sense of identity clearer, more robust and more fitting to the present.

3. Find a sense of inner peace with yourself and your past.

4. To directly see the unifying element of your life that is your presence, beyond whatever your history is.

The method of recapitulation offered here is a process of conscious contemplation that needs to come from sustained commitment and self-support and that, over time, will become automatic and automatically sustained. It is like a second awareness that, without conscious effort, continues throughout the day, and often while you are sleeping; organizing, metabolizing and integrating your everyday life.

The technique of recapitulation consists of two parts.

1. Conscious visualization

2. Letting go

What is meant by conscious visualization?

In this book we use visualization in a different way to normal usage. Visualization here is an instrument for bringing internal images (representations) into our consciousness, of ourselves, of people with whom we have relationships, of our personal history, and more generally, of the reality around us.

The process of visualization happens by degrees and manifests itself in a progressive way through associations that are predominantly subconscious.

For example, you could be asked to visualize yourself when you were an adolescent. This is a very general request that gives you lots of room to maneuver. You may have memories of yourself when you were twelve or fourteen or older. Let the images come on there own, without forcing them. Maybe the images won't come immediately or clearly, but instead, we have strong physical sensations, memories of voices or sounds, tastes, twinges in our heart, movements of the stomach or genitals.

Whatever the initial stimulus, let it be present and use your will to put it into focus and let it linger, sustaining these memories: listen, feel, look...

If you give yourself a little while and you're not in a rush, the associations will arrive spontaneously: a sound will bring forth a face and that, a sensation in your body and that, a particular emotion and thoughts of recognition and so on.

Visualization does not mean only using images but allowing an internal river of associations that include images, physical sensations, sounds, smells, emotions and thoughts, to open themselves up internally like a Pandora's box.

Returning to being adolescent, you might note that the memory of a particular jumper that was your favourite is bringing back the days on which you wore it for school, and how it made you feel protected and relaxed when you put it on. This could generate the memory that, at the same time as going to school, you had an underlying sense of discomfort and unease, a tight knot in your stomach at the idea of having to learn what didn't really interest you and having to prove your value by reciting it. Or the excitement that you felt discovering new things and new friends. Then you got home and nobody was interested in knowing how things had gone: your dad was at work and your mum in her usual state of depression... As you continue to let the visualization unravel itself you may begin to notice that there are emotions and judgments that arise regarding yourself and this time, and the people who were present. Let everything come to the surface without forcing it, without trying to put things in order or find sense.

The purpose of these visualizations is based on the awareness that we carry an enormous baggage of images from the past and that they continue to live on in our unconscious as part of our personal history, influencing our present in a subconscious way. Positive or negative as they may be, these images, as explained in Chapter II, create a filter through which we interpret reality and ourselves in it and, even more importantly, they reprogramme our present in accordance with our past.

In our context, conscious visualization has the following objectives:

1. To bring to our conscious mind, the positive and negative images of ourselves with which we identify and their physical and emotional associations.
2. To free the images of ourselves and of our parents blocked in our subconscious and in our unconscious.
3. To recognize how our attachment to inner images limits our experience of the present moment
4. To erase, or at least reduce, the attachment to these images and observe then the effect of this change in our daily lives.

A second part of the exercise of visualization is concerned with the observation of the attachment that you feel towards the images that are manifested. This can be done by asking yourself direct questions, for example: What relationship do I have with these images? Am I attached to these images? If so, how attached do I feel? Am I willing to let go of these images?

What is "letting go"? And why do it?

Our internal representations are like the dry leaves in a garden, or yesterday's clothes discarded in the bedroom. The great part of our images are not only obsolete and outmoded but, are superimposed on the present, preventing new and original experiences of the moment. Putting your house in order is an essential part of the process of conscious growth and of the possibility of living in a creative way. Freeing yourself from what you no longer need creates space for the new and helps us to become the masters of our existence and the creators of our future. It frees us from the constrictions of conditioning and opens up the road to free choice. We are lighter, more open, less guarded and burdened, less conditioned by a past made up of old images of ourselves and the world around us.

"Letting go" is a conscious process of visualization in which we see ourselves distancing ourselves from the images that we have previously called to memory or we see ourselves erasing these images. **It is fundamental to understand and remember that this act of distancing and cancellation is concerned with INTERNAL REPRESENTATIONS, with interpretations that we have used in the past and that continue to burden our present. We are NOT erasing the people or the things they represent.** Letting go of a particular image of our parents for example, doesn't mean, in any way, letting go of our parents, but of a particular set of images that we have gathered from the past. In fact, only by letting go of these past images is it possible to meet our parents (and whatever other aspect of reality) as they are today, in the present. It is like removing a pair of tinted glasses through which we've been observing a particular scene, and noting how different it is without this coloration.

Letting go is an act of love that liberates us and those that we have fixed in our internal representations. It is an act that creates space in and around us and in this space the new can manifest itself and be identified. Letting go is unclenching our fists, closed by tension and the fear of not knowing how to survive if the past should leave. Letting go is the door that leads to relaxation and happiness.

In his inauguration speech in Cape Town in 1994 the President of South Africa, Nelson Mandela read this quote

"Our deepest fear is not that we are inadequate. Our deepest fear is that we are powerful beyond measure. It is our light, not our darkness that most frightens us. We ask ourselves, Who am I to be brilliant, gorgeous, talented, fabulous? Actually, who are you not to be? You are a child of God. Your playing small does not serve the world. There is nothing enlightened about

shrinking so that other people won't feel insecure around you. We are all meant to shine, as children do. We were born to make manifest the glory of God that is within us. It's not just in some of us; it's in everyone. And as we let our own light shine, we unconsciously give other people permission to do the same. As we are liberated from our own fear, our presence automatically liberates others". [6]

[5] Castaneda, Carlos, The Second Ring of Power page 57
[6] Williamson, Marianne, from *A Return To Love: Reflections on the Principles of A Course in Miracles*

CHAPTER IV

BEYOND THE CONTRACT
OF MEDIOCRITY

*What is mediocrity? Mediocrity is the state of being in which desires,
aspirations, and inner strivings for one's highest value and meaning
in life are suppressed or dormant. Mediocrity is not the average but the
conformity to the average in the absence of desires, aspirations, and inner
strivings for one's highest value and meaning in life. Since no human
being is born with an intrinsic desire to be mediocre, but, on the contrary,
with a desire and aspiration for greatness, a mediocre person has either
to justify or to ignore his mediocrity in order to be and live with himself.
That is, he has to live a life that is untrue to and out of integrity with his
own deepest desire and aspiration.*
Yasuhiko Genku Kimura

Remembering oneself illuminates our identifications with the past
and loosens the unconscious attachment that keeps us shackled
to it. In going through this process we begin to recognize how the
personality sustains itself and a corresponding vision of the world
through some fundamental distortions. In a circular way, these
distortions are not only caused by our personality but, in turn, they
recreate and sustain the fundamental falseness of our mask through
their action.

They manifest themselves in different ways:
• Individualism substitutes the sense of our individuality which is
the sense and experience of the uniqueness of our soul.
• Constant seeking and compulsion for recognition and approval
by others substitutes direct perception of one's own intrinsic value.
• Automatic and unconscious reactivity superimposes itself on
the capacity to respond in an original and creative manner in the
present (response-ability).

• A painful tension generated by our resistance to the present takes the place of our capacity to flow, with and as a natural part of change.
• The collective hypnosis that upholds the principle of scarcity prevents the manifestation of the richness and abundance of existence.

Becoming authentic involves recognizing these distortions, becoming conscious of how they make us think, feel and act in relation to ourselves and in our relationships with others. The recognition I am speaking about is a process of understanding that happens on various levels: it is intellectual and involves the mind, it is revelation and appears in the heart, it is action and is guided by the belly; recognition is therefore a holistic process that involves diverse forms of our intelligence and all of our being.

Individualism and individuality
Individualism is generated and nurtured by the need to be special while individuality is the inner blossoming of the awareness that every human being is unique.

Individualism is the result of a fundamental lack of connection with one's own being; it is the expression of an absence, a deficiency, of not feeling oneself on a profound level and a consequent need to demonstrate, to ourselves and others, that we are special. To be special is inevitably something that exists in relation to others; it is based on making comparisons and is relative to the moment, the situation, a particular aspect of our personality that is in focus in a specific moment. To try to be special does nothing else but cause frustration, because we can be special in some things but not in everything. Wanting to be special is a left-over from infantile narcissism and the evidence of an unhealed wound, something with which everyone must deal sooner or later. Individualism, with the internal tension over being special, is the personality's attempt to sustain itself through continuous and compulsive comparisons, self-improvements, competition, being seen, being appreciated and possibly adored. Individualism claims to be superior but it is dependent and isolated, disconnected, rigid, confined and incapable of communion. Individualism is the personality's attempt to polish itself and appear special and real, rather than what it truly is: a mask.

Individualism is also an attempt to prove the substantiality and internal cohesion of ones own personality to oneself: An attempt to say to others "See, I exist", and to oneself "When the others see how special I am then I will really exist and I will be able to stop". An internal perception of inconsistency is compensated by the attention I receive and that provides me with consistency, form and substance.

Individuality, on the other hand, only appears when there is experiential recognition that who I am really is not what I appear to be. I am not the social mask that I present to the world, nor the images of myself that I hold inside and with which I identify myself. Individuality flourishes when one stops being dependent on the approval of others and of our own inner judge. Individuality is the outcome of moving our attention from the periphery of experience to the source of ourselves. It is the shift from automatic reflection on the object Me to the direct experience of I. Individuality is the external manifestation of the inner experience of absolute subjectivity, of who I am independent from my environment, my history, from the body in which I live, from the thoughts that manifest and the emotions I feel and, at the same time, as the subject of experience of all these objects. In my vision, individuality is the expression of the uniqueness of every soul and the sublime manifestation of its evolution.

On the subject of individuality the mystic Osho says:

"...when I use the word 'personality', I mean a false appearance which you have created around yourself.

Individuality is something else. Individuality does not mean something constructed and created by you, but the very nature of your being. Again, the word 'individuality' is very meaningful. It means that which cannot be divided, which is indivisible. We have an inherent intrinsic nature which cannot be divided, which is indivisible. Carl Gustav Jung chooses the word 'individuation' as one of the deepest phenomena. He said individuation is the way towards truth, towards the divine – individuation: being an individual"...

"The moment you lose the ego, the moment you discard your personalities, you become individual. This individuality is a unique phenomenon. This is unrepeatable".[7]

The experience of the individual is one of fullness, unity, integrity, inclusiveness, completeness, harmony and connection.

External approval and intrinsic value

A fundamental element of the structure of the personality is the constant dialogue between the superego (the inner judge: the figures of authority internalized in infancy, principally our parents) and the ego (the child that reacts to authority). This inner dialogue is characterized by alternating voices: one which tells us how we should and shouldn't be, how we should and shouldn't behave, what is acceptable in us and what is not, and on the other side, another which reacts to this constant pressure, refusing any interference, getting angry and fighting back or yielding, running away, giving in.

In a simplification of this internal dynamic, its fundamental modalities reveal themselves in the following way:

1. The inner judge (the internal authority) attacks and manipulates.

2. The child fights back, runs away and/or freezes.

In the internal reality of each one of us the attacks by the judge and its manipulations have dozens of shades and forms of expression depending on our personal history, the moment in which they occur and the ongoing situation. In the same way the fight, the escape and the freeze reactions take on many different forms. The point is that, independent of the form it takes, this internal confrontation is basically a closed and vicious circle of attack and reaction in which we find ourselves often entangled and incapable of getting out of. In another book I looked at this internal dynamic in detail and at ways for transforming the internal dynamic and redirecting it towards liberation from judgment (Freedom to Be Yourself). In it I emphasize how the inner judge's constant commenting and judgment of our sense of personal value as human beings and the pressure on us to carry out its principles and its interpretations if we want to be successful and be recognized by the world, is central to the dynamics. It is like having a talking grasshopper constantly sitting on our shoulder, that not only comments on EVERYTHING that happens and HOW we are and behave, but that also gives directions, opinions, advice and warnings, and terrorizes us with the tormenting doom of failure. Here we concentrate on the other essential part of this dynamic: the need for approval and recognition of the child by figures in authority. The tyrant/protector/guide that is the judge exists in a relationship of co-dependence with the victim/protected/child that, consciously or not, searches for approval and recognition.

These two parts of our psyche exist in a relationship in which they support each other in active and passive ways, peaceful and aggressive, through support and through sabotage. It's not possible to free oneself from the oppression of the superego if our infantile part continues to need its approval. In general it is quite rare for a person to be conscious of their own inner dialogue and even more so, how it includes the judge and the child: this inner dialogue is, in fact, essentially subconscious, while the energetic dynamics and the memories that sustain it are in the unconscious. It is in this way that we are able to not feel the constant pressure created by the superego: it would be very difficult to function if we were conscious of the constant background chatter in our lives all the time. At the same time, being unaware of it has disastrous repercussions in our relationships. What happens, in fact, is that the energy of this internal dialogue; an energy that cannot be contained, repressed or regulated, is projected externally, like a glass full to overflowing, and turns into the labored pursuit for other people's approval, the constant need for recognition, the compulsive necessity for an external reflection that gives us a sense of our value and even our existence.

Our identification with the personality implies not only that our value as human beings is dependent on the inner dynamics with our parents, but also with others and society in general. We have value if we dress in a certain way, if we drive a certain car, if we say certain things, if we belong to a certain race or country, if we follow a certain ideology, a certain religion and if we fight in its name.

The unique and unrepeatable creature that every one of us is – exactly the one that existence wanted in this reality and wants here in this moment – is instead reduced to an object whose value is defined externally and by others and it must struggle and struggle and struggle to prove to itself and the world that it merits the value they have awarded it, and attempt to have more.

Inquiry

Explore the theme of your personal value. How would you define it? How and when do you feel valued? Do you think that your have value independent from what others think or say about you, or not? What do you give value to in yourself and what don't you? How do you react when you realize that your value is dependent on others? How do you react when other people don't give you value?

Observe what physical sensations take place in your body when you do this exploration, whether there are tensions, contractions or whether specific parts seem to be missing, frozen or with little vitality.

Visualization

Visualize yourself when you were an adolescent and contemplate the question of your personal value. What do you remember? What events come to the surface? Let the memories arrive and run their course without forcing them and tune in to the emotions that are associated to these images. How did you create your value in your daily life? What defined it: school grades, acceptance by others, success in sport, prizes, being admired and desired, conforming, or something else? Let everything float back up to the surface and feel the associated sensations. What image of yourself appears? And how do you feel in relationship to this image?

Reaction and response

The "normal" state of functioning of the personality is reactivity, namely, to act in a compulsive and automatic way. The personality re-acts – acts again – it is repetitive and unconscious, essentially attached to past experience and fear of the new because it is unknown.

The past works like a lifeline to which we attach ourselves in order to find comfort from the fear of making mistakes and the risk of exposing ourselves. My reaction comes from the past, from memory, from what I already know and so it is always inappropriate for dealing with the present; a present that is new and in motion.

Obviously re-action lacks creativity and originality, the action is not born of the present moment and is not based on a fresh perception of the events. Re-action is the result of exercised control by our inner judge and its defense of the status quo of the personality and of its resistance to transformation. It is founded on judgments, prejudices and beliefs about ourselves and our reality. Reaction is defensive and paranoiac and always finds the cause for our unease or mistakes in external sources: *you* are the one that makes me angry so I'll strike back at you, *they* are the ones who do not understand me so I'll withdraw into myself, *you* are the one who makes me jealous so I will betray you, it is *your* fault there is unhappiness so I will make you feel guilty, and so on. Reaction not only repeats behaviors in an unconscious manner, but refuses to find the origins of these behaviors inside us: our reactions are, in fact, caused by others. In this way we always feel innocent and justified in our reactions.

When we are in contact with our being we are present, and that means we are connected to our bodies and to the sensations we feel. We are aware of our thoughts and of our emotions that come and go but we are not attached to them, we don't hold back or reject what happens, we are simply observing participants. We feel, perceive, think and take action, and everything comes from a natural flow of our presence that is responding to the present moment. Responding is spontaneous and immediate, not dictated by the past or formed by opinions, beliefs and prejudices. It is a stream of ability to respond, of our response-ability that manifests as a clarity of awareness that connects and accepts without resistance, defense, protection, anticipation or expectations. Responding happens moment by moment, it has nothing to do with the memory or control and it is not an activity constrained by fear and separate from the flow of existence. Response-ability then is not an obligation to perform, or a weight to carry around, it is the natural capacity of the soul's flow with existence in the present moment from which it is not separate. Responsibility that takes the place of reaction is not difficult, it won't make you bend in two or swell up in pride, it is in harmony with the present moment; it is light, cheerful, full of curiosity and unpredictable. Reaction resists and separates, response includes and connects.

Inquiry.
1. Can you remember moments of spontaneity? Situations in which you realize you acted in a direct manner, unrestrained, not thought out or planned? What did you feel in your body in these situations? What were the circumstances? What emotions did you feel during and afterwards? Observe the theme of spontaneity in your life and where you see yourself spontaneous and where you see yourself holding on to some sort of control. In what ways are you aware of the difference between the two forms of behavior?
2. Explore the theme of reactivity. What are the situations in which you are already aware of acting in a reactive way? How does your

reactivity manifest itself and how do you feel about your reaction? Have you tried to change and, if so, with what results? In what aspects of your life are you particularly reactive? How do you feel when you react: what physical sensations, what emotions, what thoughts and judgments take place?

Resistance and Acceptance

In "The Pearl Beyond Price" Almaas introduces a fundamental distortion in the functioning of the ego called resistance:

"Some teachings see ego in terms of its activity, which is primarily desire for future pleasure. This desire for pleasure, which entails avoidance of pain, involves rejecting the present situation and hoping for a better one. The cycle of ego activity is thus rejection, hope and desire; it is based on memories of past experience, and is directed towards the future. Thus ego, which here is an activity which resists the present moment, is clearly antithetical to the perception of the nature of reality, which involves being in the moment".[8]

Inquiry

Take a couple of minutes to absorb what you have just read and feel how it resonates inside you. Can you see resistance present in your life? Can you feel how, in most situations, the search for enjoyment pushes you compulsively to always look yonder and to escape the present moment? Can you see how when we achieve enjoyment at the same time something in you remains unsatisfied and wants more of it or wants it to last longer?

Why does the ego resist the present moment? From the point of view of its functioning, defense against pain and the search for enjoyment are motivations more than sufficient, but there is also another one.

The ego, which is the sense of identity central to the structure of the personality, lives in separation, in the belief of existing as an island separate from others and from existence and, even though that belief of separation is possibly the major cause of our suffering, it is fundamental for the survival of the structure and the associated sense of identity. No separation means no ego. No confines and boundaries mean no structure. As we have seen in the preceding chapters, the ego-identity is formed through identification with specific images of oneself and of the world, which exist as a structure in our inner space. The moment in which the confines and boundaries of the structure collapse and dissolve identification with the ego temporarily disappears. What do we look for in sexual orgasm? What do we look for in relationships, in alcohol, in adventure, in success, in spiritual search if not at least temporary relief from the usual confines through which we recognize ourselves? The story of humanity is the history of its perennial search for the dimension of non-separation, of unity, of wholeness, for a life where we don't feel small, limited, repetitive, accidental, frozen and isolated. Resistance then is a manifestation of our fear of disappearing, of dissolving away, and of the conviction that to survive we must maintain our confines and even reinforce them. In brief, resistance is the framework that holds the inner belief that I and reality exist in a dualistic way: that light is separate from dark, that good is separate from bad, beautiful from ugly, right from wrong, the body from the spirit, you from me, you from the world, you from God. In resistance we create separation, and in creating separation we create tension and suffering. In this way while, on the one hand, we seek pleasure, unconsciously we actually cause separation and suffering by trying to avoid pain. It's not difficult to see that every time we resist something this resistance generates physical, emotional or mental tension and, sooner or later, this tension generates a certain amount of suffering. We can easily see it in the way in which we function and act, in our relationships with others and in how we relate to ourselves.

Perhaps we can also see that when we stop resisting and accept things as they are the tensions melt, the stress diminishes, struggling is not necessary after all. By acceptance I don't mean a passive surrender or submission but, on the contrary, a willingness to experience reality by being completely present, curious, open, receptive to whatever comes without preconceptions and prejudices. Acceptance is a part of being response-able for our lives and in our lives. Acceptance means to begin to recognize that what we perceive as our reality is the fruit of subconscious and unconscious programmes in our minds. In some situations it is easy to recognize that we have created them through our specific programmes, in others it can be more difficult, above all when it becomes unavoidable that we assume responsibility for our own suffering. Everything that happens is substantially neutral before we superimpose our beliefs on what is acceptable and what isn't. Reality is a subjective interpretation; 'the world is a description' says Don Juan explaining to Carlos Castaneda how the personality can never have an objective view of the world. A description that we repeat to ourselves for years and years and that we now take to be true. Accepting what is takes us out of a fixed description and opens us up to the moment we are living and its absolute originality and newness. This moment, this line that you are reading, the sensations that you are feeling, the light around you and the sense of the weight of your body and your breath going in and out, NONE OF THIS HAS EVER HAPPENED BEFORE. Every description is impossible, only direct experience, unprejudiced and of the moment, is real. Each description is just a story. Acceptance is therefore a plunge into the 'here and now' and when I accept the 'here and now' the limits imposed by the description that I have created in the past have neither sense nor meaning.

My vision of reality is that only ONE energy exists in the universe, aware of itself and of everything. In the awareness of its own total inclusiveness this energy is secure, happy and in peace and this makes us feel secure, happy and in peace with our true nature. The recognition and reconnection with the conscious nature of Being induce a state of unity and contentment, while the identification with the conditioning we have undergone and the programme of the personality creates division, isolation and suffering. In this hypnosis of suffering the universe is imperfect and hostile and so there is always something to be done, somewhere to go, something to achieve, something to improve or something to avoid in order to be happy.

Scarcity and abundance

The inevitable consequence of believing we exist as reduced entities, limited, divided, conditioned by the past, dependent on the superego, preoccupied by others' opinions, separate from existence, intent on resisting what happens in the present while struggling in every way to control the future.. does this description of the personality seem too extreme? I really hope not, because, if you look honestly and carefully at everyday life you can easily find all these ingredients. Then another, that inevitable: the absolute conviction that everything is scarce. The belief in scarcity is the thorn in the side of our personality, the cause of our daily worries, desperation and our core questioning and uncertainty. Not only is life hostile, not only do I have to struggle in every way possible to make things happen, to manipulate myself and reality so that my dreams and desires might come true, not only must I get by in the middle of conflict and delusions, competition and frustrations but, on top of it, I am also told and made to believe that my chances of success are very small because everything is scarce and "inevitably few get the prize while the majority lose". The principle of scarcity is at the basis of all social life and is re-proposed to us untiringly through politics, the economy, philosophy and religion.

Everywhere we look there are the chosen few and the excluded and logical reasons and rationalizations that justify that reality. Love is scarce so be careful who you give it to, happiness is scarce so hang onto it as long as you possibly can, richness is scarce so fight for it and don't share it, faith is scarce and few will go to heaven, sincerity is scarce so don't trust anyone, sexuality is scarce so be satisfied with what you've got... you can go on and on. And since everything is scarce we have to struggle, wrestle, compete, fight our way to the top, exclude, renounce, hack out, diminish, look down,

49

belittle. The principle of scarcity is a virus that infects us from birth. Nevertheless, when we look in the eyes of a baby what we see is obvious and unmistakable; what the baby brings to the world is an abundant river of potentiality, a living reflection of the perfection of the universe.

Almaas calls the original state of a baby, a state of "primary self-realization" and it indicates a sense of essential completeness and not division, a state of natural and immediate presence. This state disappears over time due to conditioning and adaptation to the environment:

"The soul loses awareness of its wholeness through the loss of the immediacy of experience, which results from experiencing itself through past impressions. The loss of immediacy is identical with the loss of awareness of presence, and since presence is the 'glue" that unifies all aspects of experience, wholeness is gone. The baby loses her primary self-realization (and her primary narcissism) as she begins to experience herself as an object. An increasing veil composed of memories (and reaction-induced results or consequences) intervenes between the subject – the self – and the object. This duality gradually transforms the infant's experience in such a way that she ultimately loses her identification with the sense of presence. As the infant develops an identity situated in dimensions of experience superficial to her essential presence, she loses her capacity to simply be herself".[9]

The completeness is lost due to the abandonment of presence, this abandonment creates division between me and objects and this division creates an inner sense of separation and loss. This loss is painful so I look for something outside which can make me complete: a lover, a car, a job, an idea, a new bag or an ice-cream, a flash of inspiration or success... something that, for just one moment, makes me feel whole again and satisfied. Since everyone lives with the loss of something then it seems to be logical to the collective hypnosis that this loss isn't caused by an inner distortion but, obviously, from the fact that what we look for is limited, scarce, difficult to attain or achieve. Everything is turned upside down: since existence is scarce therefore I feel the loss, and as I feel this loss it means that I'm not complete, and... this is my destiny, so it is better to resign myself, and... it's up to you to add here what your inner judge says at this point.

Inquiry

Explore the theme of scarcity in your daily life. What are your beliefs in merit? Where does the belief that life is scarce affect you the most? Observe what your beliefs are regarding material and spiritual richness, how you establish confines and limits to your abundance and the possibility of abundance. What practical effects manifest as result of your believing in scarcity? What happens in your body when you undergo this exploration and what type of emotions emerge? Do you find yourself in situations of conflict with yourself or others on this theme?

In praise of rebellion

Rebellion is an effervescence in the soul, a creative whirlwind of awareness, and the natural drive of evolutionary instinct that takes form. To stop rebelling means to stop evolving, which means an attempt to halt this natural force; a natural force that continuously seeks self-expression in the present moment, creating what I am moment by moment in a new, original and unpredictable way. To stop rebelling means betraying the fundamental pulsing of desire and of the life force that every one of us manifests in a way that is unique and unrepeatable. It means betraying the great Cosmic Plan that has brought us to this planet and wants us here and now as its living senses, present and luminous. Ceasing to rebel means conforming to the contract of mediocrity that society asks you to sign every day in the name of survival and to turn your back to Life. Ceasing to rebel means to not risk making mistakes, to not take responsibility for our lives, to righteously point out the straw in another's eye, unaware of the plank in our own. Ceasing to rebel means renouncing the pursuit of truth and adapting yourself to whatever truth is offered, imposed, sold to you. Ceasing to rebel means swallowing others' truths and then complaining because we can't digest them.

Continuing to hold oneself inside the structure of the personality involves enormous fatigue. We are so used to doing it that we're not even aware of how much tension it produces, how many compromises we keep making, how much we forsake what we truly feel in the name of survival. We have been habituated since childhood to control and deaden our vitality, in all its forms, and to make ourselves small. We live, literally, within a band of energy that's incredibly limited, where any extreme is unacceptable: too much sex isn't allowed, too much happiness, too much attention, too much self-value, too much love; we can dream, but not really live.

Rebelling, then, is a choice for life, for truth and for the adventure of discovery. WHO AM I REALLY? Who is hiding behind the image I show to the world? What is life if I free myself from the concepts with which I define it and stop shrinking and making myself small in order to adapt myself to these concepts?

[7] Osho, The Ultimate Alchemy, vol. I, chapter 2
[8] Almaas A.H., The Pearl Beyond Price, page.20
[9] Almaas A.H., The Point of Existence, page.41

CHAPTER V

RECOGNISING RELATIVE TRUTH

Always and never

Has it ever occurred to you how often we say "always" and "never"? Have you ever sometimes thought that what you were saying was impossible? Have you ever begun to wonder whether perhaps you were lying with that "always' or "never"? Have you felt the impulse to correct what you are saying and remove that "always'" or "never" and maybe put: "sometimes" or "often" or "frequently"? Do you get agitated and absolutely convinced that it's true, it's definitely like this, he has NEVER loved me, she has NEVER cared for me, this relationship has ALWAYS been difficult, it will ALWAYS be a failure, I will NEVER be successful...

Inquiry

Stop for a moment and listen to the sound of these words and observe the energy that they support. Stop right now and take a moment to bring back to memory recent conversations with friends, colleagues, wives or husbands, children, parents, and remember when you have used this ALWAYS or this NEVER and in what context and feel the energy behind the words. Explore the physical sensations that come up while remembering these events, one by one.

Feel whether there is tension, feel whether there is a sense of righteous indignation, the enduring affirmation of a wrongdoing, whether there is a sense of dissatisfaction and resignation, whether your backbone becomes rigid or compressed. Observe with curiosity and participation, in a non-judging manner, what effects saying ALWAYS and NEVER have on you.

The need for certainty

"Always" and "never" are powerful words that hide profound

implications and generate reactions and repercussions. But first of all they are false words when referred to experience: existentially false. They are words that generalize and carry existence to extreme trying to create a continuity and certainty that don't exist. They are words that separate us from ourselves, from existence and from the other. Always and never try to hide the precariousness of the present moment and the change that is in action now, and now, and now, moment after moment. Always and never try to stop the river that is flowing creating the illusion that it's possible to control the future pledging something we know we can't maintain. Always and never are words that our inner judge uses to judge us and to judge the world around us: you are never good enough, you always do the wrong things, no-one will ever love you, in the world you need to always struggle, you must always win, you never surrender, always be strong, don't ever make mistakes, always tell the truth, and so on. To the internal pressure and manipulation carried out by the superego responds from the other side the unconscious reactivity and narcissism of the child inside us that never wants to listen, that always wants to do what he wants to do, that never has time for the others, that always wants pleasure and never sadness, that never wants to grow up and wants to always remain a child, that never wants to be alone, that always wants to be loved and accepted... In this world made up of always and never the incomprehension and conflict are inevitable, the stiffening of positions and of confines a foregone result, the defense of our own opinions at all cost indication of character instead of infantile stubbornness.

Always and never are words existentially impossible because as it has been said, "the only certain thing in the world is change".

The attempt to stop the world that unconsciously we put in motion using the words always and never is the result of our inner uncertainty and above all the sensation of loss of solidity and integrity, maintenance and support. This loss of inner certainty isn't caused,as we like to think, from the fact that everything constantly changes, but from the loss of connection with our true nature and the identification with the personality and that is with something that deep inside we know to be limited, learned from others and fundamentally false. When we think about resolving our problems of insecurity and uncertainty struggling to control our lives, not only is our attention aimed in the wrong direction, towards the outside, but we are bound to fail. For a moment perhaps we can delude ourselves of having our lives and future under control because we have a job, a family, a bank account, a house, a car, a certain role and certain tasks, because we are loved and recognized, but if we look carefully and we are honest with ourselves, the illusion lasts a short time and we realize that each one of these things can change any moment and then we come to a standstill and once again we have to deal with uncertainty and unpredictability. In reality, the more we struggle to control ourselves, others, and the world around us, the more we are stressed and tense, the closer we are to the possibility or actuality of failing and the frustration of our attempts. This existential uncertainty isn't new and does not appertain to us alone, in the history of humanity poets, artists, philosophers, mystics have spoken about it. The big difference is that in today's reality the rhythm of change and the consequent collapse and transformation of social structures has accelerated enormously and this speed often leaves us breathless and disoriented.

Beyond the conflict.

When we use the words always and never, unconsciously we create a state of conflict whether inside us, with others or with reality in general.

An essential understanding in overcoming and dissolving these conflicts is comprehension and acceptance of relative truth.

Relative truth relates to what happens to a particular person in a particular situation and at a particular moment. For example the relative truth of this moment is that you are reading this book, that your body has a specific position while sitting, standing or lying down, still or walking, that the light around you has a particular quality and intensity, and that everything occurs in a particular environment around you and so on; we can always go on to refine the description of the things that make up your relative experience of this moment in this situation. And we can also see that this truth regards this moment and that a moment ago something was different: for example the words you were reading or the position of your hand, or the noises around you etc. All this is simple enough to accept even if, when we find ourselves in discussion with others, we often try however, to convince ourselves about events that "the facts" were in a certain way and not in another. The most important aspect of relative truth is the inside one - which is completely subjective - and has to do with the way in which you experience yourself as you read, this book, these words, with this body position, with this light and these noises around you and these physical sensations and maybe these thoughts and these emotions. What you experience is YOUR way of experiencing this moment. Every moment of which you are aware is your personal way of experiencing what happens, and when you find yourself telling others about your experience what you tell them will be a subjective interpretation of events and completely personal and biased. It will be a relative truth to you and the way in which you experienced, interpreted and remembered those particular events. Also note how every experience from beginning to end is lived though the filters of our conditioning and our personal history: we see, feel and sense only what is allowed to be sensed and that fits our personality's values.

Inquiry
Explore recent situations in which you have found yourself in conflict with others regarding the reconstruction of the "facts" of a particular situation, regarding the interpretation of events, the perception of situations, occurrences and other people. What produces the conflict? What effect does it have to feel different and have contradictory points of view? What do you feel in your body when your version is refused, slated or ridiculed? How do you react

to opinions and interpretations different to your own? Do you try to be right? Do your refuse to argue? Do you reject the other because "he doesn't understand"? Do you pretend to agree? Observe the modality of your behavior in relation to the theme of "relativity" of experience and of the perception of reality.

When, through observation of your behaviors and your beliefs, you become aware of how often you try to affirm as absolute and general truth those that are instead relative truths then it will become clear to you also your attachment to your particular interpretation of reality and how this attachment derives from your need to feel safe. You will also see how the attachment produces an infinity of conflicts on all levels otherwise avoidable. In most situations of disagreement it is enough to remind yourself that a point of view and interpretation of facts is personal and relative and that there isn't one wrong and one right but two, or more, different. Instead of closing your mind and your heart against others in the name of "right" truth and "correct" interpretation, we can open ourselves to the possibility of difference and diversity, to tolerance and the possibility of taking on a different point of view, that which common sense calls "putting yourself in the others' shoes". At the same time, the acknowledgement of relative truth turns into a mighty engine of enrichment of our experience and integration of our unconscious as well as others' points of view. We are literally richer when instead of excluding we give ourselves the permission to look at reality with the eyes of others.

PART III
TOWARDS YOUR
AUTHENTIC SELF

CHAPTER VI

RADICAL COMPASSION
IS CREATIVE ACTION

The substitute life is a very narrow way of living. This narrowness is rooted in our need to feel comfortable, to cling to what is familiar and safe. To avoid experiencing the anxious quiver at the core of our being, where we might feel the chaos of uncertainty or the pain of unhealed wounds, we weave a protective cocoon of beliefs and identities. Unfortunately, living in this way also cuts us off from the vastness of our True Nature, our naturally open heart.
Ezra Bayda

Right understanding

Compassion is the flourishing of right understanding that comes from the heart. Right understanding isn't right in opposition to one that is wrong but it is right because it is without veils, not filtered or distorted by the past, by concepts and conditioning. It's right because it is immediate, without judgments and prejudices. It is right because it is an expression of Being and not of the personality. It is right because it is not dualist and doesn't separate but unites and includes.

Right understanding occurs in three fundamental centers in the human being: it is clarity in the mind, revelation in the heart and impeccable gut action. When we observe reality through the eyes of the heart it reveals itself in its intrinsic goodness and abundance. The screen that divides light from shade disappears and reality appears, not divided and not dividable. The heart is empathetic and without defense and has the capacity to feel, absorb and integrate all the pain that there is in us and others. The illusion, that happiness exists without pain, dissolves. The idea that pain can be avoided and, on the contrary, we understand that an essential element of our humanity is the capacity to feel it, in ourselves and others. We understand that this capacity isn't only at the base of tenderness and of taking care of ourselves but it is also an indispensable part of our sensibility and that without this ability we would be superficial, barren, incomplete. Our capacity to feel, recognize and integrate our pain and that of others enables us to grow emotionally and, paradoxically, to open ourselves also to greater and greater levels of pleasure and bliss. When the awareness, slowly and courageously, brings light to the depths of our unconscious, inevitably we find ourselves meeting all the materials that we repressed in infancy through fear of punishment or because it was judged to be unacceptable and to be refused, for fear of the power of our urges and passions or for that need of approval and the necessity to belong that distances us from our individuality. In resisting our unconscious matter and in the continual effort to keep it unconscious, we continue to recreate pain and tension. **However, pain is not intrinsic to this repressed material. It is our resistance to this matter that generates pain and it is our repression of this pain that causes tension.**

Through continuous self-judgment we refuse the totality of what we are, we divide ourselves into light and shadow to then hide the shadow-side and anxiously try to convince ourselves and others that we are only light: that in us there is no anger, greed, jealousy, arrogance, envy and all those other horrible things that we call our trash. Why are we surprised then if we feel exhausted? Or paranoid and afraid at the thought that others will discover what we are hiding?

Right understanding in the heart means opening yourself to the experience of the moment in its totality, embracing everything there is, above all the vulnerability that we feel when the experience is out of our control, out of our capacity to rationalize, when we feel overwhelmed, fragile, bruised, lost. Right understanding in the heart means accepting not knowing, to not have true answers that are the fruit of our experience in the present and not what our inner judge says, from repetition of the past or of things we have read.

Right understanding is an infusion of curiosity and innocence. Right understanding occurs when we are willing to feel our resistance and the tension that develops and how it separates us from ourselves, from others and the experience of the moment.

"...resisting something is one good way to preserve it in the form that we experienced it to begin with. We resist hoping to get rid of it, but what we are actually doing is encapsulating it and keeping it in its original form or expression."..." Resistance implies a division inside of us. It signals that we are not recognizing that what is arising is a manifestation of our own consciousness, of our awareness. When hatred arises in us, for example, or fear, it is our soul, our consciousness, taking that form at that time for a reason we perhaps don't understand yet. If we are able to allow the fear or hate, embrace it, hold it, and feel it fully in its totality – in all its texture, color, and vividness – we will give it the space to be itself. And that will happen naturally because it is the nature of our True nature to move, to unfold, to illuminate itself, and to reveal what it is about".[10]

Accepting what happens inside ourselves as an expression of our soul manifesting itself and observing how the significance of that manifestation becomes evident if we don't resist, sowing the seeds for right comprehension and those seeds flower in compassion: Compassion for ourselves and for others. As soon as we give ourselves the permission to be ourselves in all our reality, we immediately give the same permission to others and in this act of liberation we recognize our uniqueness and that of every other human being.

In search of the lost heart

I don't know how many dozens of times I was told, first in my youth and then as an adult, that I didn't have a heart. And I also remember the discomfort of hearing those words and the confusion, the frustration and the impotence. I felt misunderstood and judged and usually my first reaction was to close myself and to pretend I was untouched. With time I realised that these words pointed to something, something that I could continue to ignore or that, instead, I could try to recognize and feel. The first thing that became clear was that there was an obvious difference between how others perceived me in certain situations and the way in which I perceived myself. I needed a good deal of time to admit and accept that the others could be in good faith and didn't necessarily want to hurt me and that probably they were trying to tell me something in such a way that it made me feel bad. Then I became aware that I was feeling bad because inside I was also saying the same things: you haven't got a heart, you haven't got a heart! At the same time I felt that there was something that was hiding itself and that this hiding was creating a sort of rigidity within me and that this rigidity was perceived externally as seriousness and toughness.

At that point instead of getting angry and reacting to what the others were saying I began to try and understand what was inside me that was attacking me using these same words that the others were using, and discovered my superego. I realised that behind the attacks there were messages my inner judge was giving me: "be careful of opening yourself up too much, you'll get hurt" and "don't lower your guard because they'll think you're weak" and "keep a safe distance, if not they'll attack you". And then I understood that the real issue wasn't that I didn't have a heart but that I was afraid to open it and, for the first time, I felt with absolutely clarity a metal shield that was covering my chest not permitting others to enter and behind which I was hiding. What was I hiding? It took several years to find the answer.

Becoming aware of how I hid myself and sensing that there was fear behind the shield, for a long time I dedicated myself to reconnecting myself with the strength within me, a strength that I always felt in my belly, sensing that this force could sustain me in facing fear. This strength was a sense of grounding and centering, solidity and intuitive action, the capacity to be on my own and support myself. This strength was something in me that I knew and on which I could count on and that I knew how to nourish: perhaps, if I felt completely certain of myself and safe, one day

I would be able to lower the shield and open my heart, I said to myself. For years I dedicated myself to Martial Arts and to centering and grounding meditations while continuing to feel the desperation of not being able to completely open up my heart and curiosity and the frustration of not knowing what was hidden. I put everything into this. I was a warrior in search of myself and the truth. And in putting everything into that, without realizing it, while my strength and passion were growing, grew also my identification with the need to strive, the attachment to the intensity and the need to prove to myself that I was a seeker of truth... at all costs.

Something began to give way one day when I suddenly realised how much pressure I was putting myself under and had put myself under in the name of enlightenment and to knowing myself. I took account that while, on the one hand, I didn't have the minimum idea of where I was heading, on the other hand, I continued to want to control how I got there, how I searched, and that in the end I had idealized a certain way of "searching for truth". I also realised that in that idealization I had fixed myself to a precise image of myself: the warrior, unfortunately still without a heart. I also realised that the struggle that I had undergone and the honesty of my pursuit had created fantastic results: a very strong rapport with my body, a simple and innocent passion for awareness, a clear connection with my roots and the capacity to explore. By this time I had become a master of intention, now perhaps it was the moment to open myself and embrace everything I found without discriminating and trying to keep things together: maybe to fall apart, to let go, to get lost and feel myself without footholds and a safety net was possible.

Finally, in those years, one of the names given to me by Osho was: Samarpan, namely surrender, it began to make sense. And so I began to surrender little by little. I began by handing myself over to Osho, my master, and he asked me to surrender myself to my need for love and my fear of intimacy, to surrender myself to my anger, to surrender myself to not knowing, to surrender myself to my desire for contact, to surrender myself to my weakness and, above all, to surrender myself to my vulnerability. He asked me directly and through the women I loved and the friends around me and the situations that life created. While the shield that covered my chest loosened, I began to listen to the voice of my heart and hear what was hidden behind the shield: the nobility of weakness and the sweetness of vulnerability and the immensity of my desire for fusion with myself, with others, with the world and with God. It was then that "compassion", a word for a long time rejected and despised, began to make sense to me that I was beginning to feel compassion for myself and my battle and my longings and my fears and the aggressions of my judge and the isolation and the needs and the melancholy behind my rage and all that makes me human.

Osho says:

"Anger arises in man's heart if his heart is not balanced. If the same heart becomes balanced, then the energy which begins as anger starts transforming into compassion. Compassion is the transformation of anger."…"Compassion does not arise through the destruction of anger: it is attained through the transformation of anger. Compassion is not the destruction of anger, it is anger that has become tuned and musical. So if you are opposed to anger and try to destroy it, then you are trying to destroy the musical instrument"[11]

Creating reality with the kindness of love

What I call: "radical compassion", is a method for activating, sustaining, applying and expressing right understanding in everyday life. It is a practice that requires presence, generosity and intention. The practice of radical compassion is the fount of creative action. Because in order for an action to be creative it needs to be liberated from the past, even though it is instructed by it. Such an action comes from inclusion and conscious integration of our past as it is liberated from the superego's resistance to transformation and from the reactivity of the narcissistic child. The practice of radical compassion includes three elements that sustain and nourish one another:

1. Practicing holding attention and presence in the body.
2. Consciously defending against the inner judge by saying YES to everything that there is.
3. Opening oneself up to truth through the practice of self-inquiry.

Practicing presence

Practicing presence means recognizing that everything that happens to us whether internally or externally, in our relationships with others, has some manifestation in our physical body. Every emotion, every perception, every thought, every change of mood or sentiment, is associated to some kind of physical sensation: as long as we exist in a physical body, everything we experience in any given moment also exists on a physical level in our body. And our physical body is always in the present, the here/now. Therefore practicing presence is a way of using our body like an anchor in the present and consciously begin to be here/now with all that we are: thoughts, ideas, emotions, sentiments, desires, etc. Practicing presence is the key for recognizing the totality of our experience as it happens in the present, even if it is the effect of memories, concepts, opinions, or of the past in general. Practicing presence is also the basic ground on which we build our capacity to access wider, more profound, and higher levels of our Being, beginning with our unconscious. This fundamental ground is what sustains us when the judge attacks us, when we feel overpowered by the mind, when our emotions make us explode, when we are lost and we feel defenseless: knowing what I am standing on is absolutely fundamental. And this ground is here/now, in the present, and I can feel it if I listen to my body that is, also it, here/now.

Therefore feel, listen, observe, carefully identify what your body is saying in this and in every moment. Let a part of your consciousness be constantly in tune with the sensations that manifest themselves, feel the network of information that runs in the rhythm of your heart, in your nervous system, the movement of your muscles, in the activity of your glands, the tensions and relaxation, in weight and lightness, in the changes of temperature, in the echoes of your breathing, in the expansion and contraction, in the uploading and offloading of energy, in the thousands and thousands of ways in which your body is alive now, right here.

Defending yourself from the judge

In my book on the inner judge, I dealt with two basic techniques for conscious defense from attacks by the superego and I invite you to practice them with total participation. There is no freedom while ever we are dependent on the approval of others, inside and out. Wanting and looking for approval is one thing, being a slave to it and feeling insecure and lesser if we don't receive it is another. Everyone wants recognition and positive reflections from the world for the simple fact that when we are given affection and care, we grow better and almost effortlessly, it is our dependency on approval that makes life so often exhausting and difficult, if not impossible, to be trusting in our own capacity and resources. In the practice of radical compassion the way in which we defend ourselves from the judge is simply saying yes to all existence in all ways in which it manifests itself. It is a yes without reserve, a yes that accepts and includes, that opens up to the possibility that everything that happens comes from a vast and unknown source, much more intelligent than our personality. That considers the possibility that the universe is benevolent also when we encounter pain and difficulty. That responds to the heart and not only the head and the need for control. Saying yes to ourselves, to our shadow, fear, resistance, limitation, to attachment and need, to weakness, not only expands our perception within and towards the world, but is also an act of courage that openly affirms what all the wise men and mystics of human history have said: I AM ALL THERE IS AND WHOLE. Including all of myself I integrate myself and grow with all my parts: I re-member. When the judge doesn't find resistance and doesn't know who to attack and, on the contrary is accepted, it feels initially disorientated and then, slowly, it calms down, leaving you free to be yourself.

In this space that opens up internally our relationship begins to change with the figures of authority from our infancy, in particular our parents, and it becomes possible to let go of the frozen images of our past and above all the suffering that they entail.

Hunting for truth

On the journey to self-discovery, the method of inquiry is what, more than any other, manifests our love for the truth and our curiosity.

Differently to the classic Buddhist method of observation, inquiry is much more active because consciously we dive into the present moment and open it through exploration, questioning, and a dynamic participation to the emerging of reality. We not only want to know the truth and observe it manifest itself and unfold, but also, with our questions, we allow our comprehension to shed light on the meaning. The more our questions are deeply felt and in tune with the moment, the more the truth responds and makes itself obvious, evident. The meaning of each moment is revealed and, as that happens, we feel clarity in our minds, connection in our hearts and certainty in our bellies.

"Inquiry is a dynamic functioning of our consciousness, of our soul, that has to be flexible, responsive, and playful for it to be truly intelligent. It has to be inspired by intelligence and informed by understanding. As you inquire, you need to use your intelligence, and you need to apply whatever understanding you have to the experience of the moment. Inquiry is not a matter of asking a question haphazardly; all questions have to be asked in an organic way. That is what intelligence is: an organic and appropriate responsiveness to each situation". [12]

[10] Almaas A.H., The Unfolding Now, pag.39
[11] Osho, The Inner Journey, chap.7
[12] Almaas A.H., Spacecruiser Inquiry, pages 55, 56

CHAPTER VII

SOME TECHNIQUES THAT WILL
SUPPORT YOU ON YOUR JOURNEY

The techniques that you will find in this chapter are powerful and effective. They are simple and direct and tackle fundamental aspects of the self-hypnosis through which we keep ourselves enslaved to the past and false identity. As with all techniques it is essential to remember that the more you use them the more they work and so your full and ongoing commitment is a must. The techniques are:

1. Remember that what you call reality is only an interpretation.
2. If I say yes to myself...
3. Let go of the suffering of those you love and of your own.
4. Tonglen.
5. Put yourself in the other's shoes.

The world is a description.
What we call "reality" is nothing more than a description, a point of view. When the point of view changes, the interpretation changes and with it the description of reality. You only have to observe the difference of perceptions of the same events by different people to recognize the simple, and at the same time difficult to accept, obviousness of such a claim. It certainly will help if we have an understanding of what is relative truth and also of our egoic need for making our point of view an absolute. This technique is very simple and direct: it just involves remembering that what we call "reality" is an interpretation of the moment relative to us who are experiencing it. This remembering, not only enables us to accept different descriptions offered by other people but enables us to continue verifying how attached we are to our position and the investment

we make in wanting to be right at all costs. It also gives us a degree of flexibility in our understanding of the continuous movement of transformation, a flexibility that proves to be indispensable when we are stuck in the conviction that the reality that we experience is fixed and the only one. We can also note how the description of the world is underpinned by our inner dialogue and, specifically by the internal dynamic between the superego and the ego. This dynamic, that reflects our original relationship with our parents, re-proposes and re-affirms a description of reality borrowed from our family environment and is destined to stay infantile and repetitive until we empty out its foundations. The claim that reality is a description is an ever-growing confirmation also made by modern science, and especially by quantum physicists. In time, remembering can open new ways of perceiving also that physical reality that we take for granted, the reality of the space in which we exist, and the reality of time and of its presumed motion.

The technique
It is extremely simple: when you realize you're intensely involved in a conflict, whether with yourself or someone else or with a situation, remember that what you perceive, in all its shades, with all its value and concepts, with its emotions and opinions etc, everything, absolutely everything, is your interpretation. Take a deep breath and observe what happens inside when the interpretation is recognized for what it is. After a little take another deep breath and visualize all this interpretation while it is melting away, like snow under the sun, or decomposing into minute particles that are whipped away by the wind.

If I say yes to myself...
We begin to take account of how much we refuse ourselves, how much we push our experiences away, how much we say no to what we hear, think, feel, see. How is it possible to be really ourselves if we continually deny a part of the experience that we are living, if

we deny our jealousy, fear, anger and greed because some others, or perhaps many others, have told us that it is wrong to feel what we feel. The fact that everyone feels these emotions is conveniently left aside in the name of sanctity and an anemic and castrated kind-heartedness. Nevertheless all the great saints of Christianity, of Buddhism, of Islamism have demonstrated profound human qualities and, in most cases they don't make claims of having negated or refused these emotions, but rather of having accepted them and of having simply stopped, through that acceptance, of attaching themselves to them. The focal point is on the attachment not on the experience itself. The focal point is on the unconscious action that results in our attachment to anger or to greed that otherwise, in itself, is neutral and impotent. It is our energy that gives them their life and produces the consequences. So let's begin saying yes to EVERYTHING that we find inside.

The technique
To be used every time that you feel the need and, above all when you feel that you are struggling to be different from how you really feel. The technique works in this way: in those situations in which you tend to say no, instead of denying yourself, stop and use the phrase "If I say yes to myself...." and fill in the dots with whatever comes up. Use the technique only internally like a sensor and observe how you *would* be, what you *would* do, what you *might* feel if you said yes in that situation. Don't act, simply be aware.

Turn your back to suffering: Understanding DUKKHA
To the rational mind, the attachment to suffering seems a complete absurdity and, if we want to be purely logical, it is. But how do we explain then, the fact that we continue to repeat behaviors that generate suffering in ourselves and in others? Is it possible that a "loyalty" to suffering exists? Is it possible that this devotion is unconscious and totally automatic in its functioning? Is it possible that this devotion is justified by concepts that we have regarding

life, that: "life is suffering", "each one of us must carry his cross" or in the case of Americans, "no pain, no gain"? Is it possible that there is a powerful programme in our unconscious that prevents us from seeing life as something happy and adventurous, to explore and enjoy? The original term used by Buddhists in the expression of the First Noble Truth is DUKKHA. Dukkha was often translated as "suffering" and so the First Noble Truth sounds like: "Life is suffering", and also this seemed to support us in our collective hypnosis. And naturally also in the struggle to run away or put an end to this suffering.

But Zen proposes a different interpretation: the significance of the word Dukkha, in fact, represents a situation in which "the axle of a wheel is out of center". Obviously, you know what happens to a wheel that starts turning with a misaligned axle: it jerks, it jams, wobbles, slows down then accelerates; it blocks, vibrates uncontrollably, and so on. This is the condition of man identified with the personality and separate from his true nature: The separation, the division, the repression, struggle, denial, prejudice: All this is Dukkha.

On the basis of this understanding we can then shift our attention from desire to avoid suffering (useless and destined to failure) to the fact of finding the most effective and personal ways of returning the axle to the center of the wheel and going back to having contact with our center as individuals.

The technique

In this case our attention is focused on how our attachment to images of ourselves, our parents and of other people we love that are frozen in our minds provoke a constant state of friction and unconscious frustration that result in disharmony and tension.

This techniques works through visualization and don't forget that, towards the end of the second chapter, you will find an explanation on how to use visualization.

Find a peaceful place where you know you won't be disturbed and dedicate at least twenty minutes or so for this technique. Sit in a comfortable position with your eyes closed, let your breathing become relaxed and natural. Connect with your body: feel how you are sat, how you are breathing, the temperature of your hands, the sensations of your skin as it touches your clothes and relax the muscles in your face, your shoulders, your stomach.

Internally, choose a situation with another person (or other people) that has caused you displeasure, where there was conflict, that you feel is unresolved or simply stagnant and begin to visualize the other person (or other people). Observe carefully what you feel when you look at the other person with your inner eyes: what impression does the other person make, what emotions do you think the other person is feeling, what thoughts emerge, how does the other person look, what is their mood and how does that affect you? In particular focus your attention on their suffering and how you perceive this. How does this suffering look to you: is it like a solid wall that separates you, is it a haze and a sensation of helplessness, is it cold, is there anxiety or pain, is it like having a dry throat full of glass splinters, is there outrage, is it thick, is it dark, or something else? Look carefully at how you perceive the suffering of others and consciously avoid judging or commenting on what you see. Feel what is happening in your body as you visualize. When you feel ready, refer inside to the person (or people) that you see and say: "My dear (name)... I am very fond of you, but I can't continue to support your suffering". Then turn around inside and move away.
For a few minutes simply observe what happens inside you then repeat the same sequence with yourself. Visualize yourself in front of yourself and observe what your suffering looks like in relation to that person (and those people). Don't rush yourself, sense precisely what characteristics that suffering has in that situation; what thoughts are associated with it, what physical sensations, what emotions, what images, and so on. When you feel ready, repeat the previous words in relation to yourself and then move away. Spend a few minutes staying in contact with what happens as a result of this experience.

This technique is deeply effective as it cleans out old unconscious images of ourselves and others from our system. Repeat it again every time you feel blocked within yourself or by some relationship: let the past images go, they are just interpretations!

Tonglen

The technique that follows is based on an ancient Tibetan Buddhism practice called Tonglen: 'tong' means to send and 'len' means to receive.

Contrary to the previous technique, in which we distance ourselves from suffering, in this technique we absorb the suffering and share our love and our happiness. The technique can be used either with another person or on your own and is based on visualization and breathing.

The technique

1. On your own
Visualize yourself in your usual suffering: when you feel alone, abandoned, useless, confused, unvalued, angry, ill or afraid. As you become conscious of your own suffering in daily life feel your heart warming itself in sympathy and understanding for that suffering and opening up to the will to help your self to be free. Imagine the suffering that you see is a dark cloud, and that with every breath, you absorb it into your heart illuminated by your courage and your compassion. Each time you breathe out send unconditional love, joy and acceptance.

2. With others
Begin by contemplating the suffering of others and by connecting yourself with your heart and its capacity to feel and transform. Visualize the person (or people) in front of you and listen, observe their suffering and they experience it in their daily life. Note how, in pain, we are all the same and that only the ego believes that no-one suffers quite like us; the ego in fact tries to make us feel special even

in our suffering. Look at the person and say to him: "I suffer too, just like you, I too am human". Breathe in the darkness and give back light from your heart.

Practice this technique whenever your want and for however long you need.

Putting yourself in another's shoes

As old as the world and ordinarily wise. This technique is extremely effective in situations in which we find ourselves in conflict with others and we are absolutely convinced we're right and, obviously, that the other person is wrong. To use this technique it's not necessary to give up your own point of view or necessarily accept the other's point of view. If you find yourself doggedly trying to defend your position or opinion at all costs then... this is the technique you should use.

The technique

As soon as you realize that you're getting defensive or extremely aggressive in a conflict with someone else simply stop, ask yourself why you are so attached to your position, and whether it could help you to open up your awareness to different points of view. If the answer is yes then use this technique: close your eyes and breathe deeply giving yourself space to let go your tensions as much as possible.

Visualize the person with whom you are in conflict standing in front of you about three or four meters away. Also visualize yourself standing up and then begin to walk towards the other person step by step, with the intention of putting yourself in the other person's shoes more and more with every step you take. As you get nearer begin to transform yourself into the other person and, little by little, become the other person. Your body changes into their body, the sound of your voice becomes theirs, the clothes you're wearing become theirs and you continue transforming until you feel you are the other person completely. At that point you have disappeared and only the other person remains, who is now you. Experience how it feels to be the other person: feel the sensations in your body, the thoughts that pass through your mind and the emotions you feel...let all the new information surge up spontaneously inside you along with your new position in the conflict in which you're involved. Note the different perspective and everything associated with you: in your gut, in your heart and in your head. When you feel that you have absorbed and taken on the new perspective begin the inverse process, let go of the other person and return to yourself, step by step, carefully, feeling how it is to let the other go and return to being yourself. Before opening your eyes, when you feel you have completely returned, look at the other person and internally thank them. Take a couple of deep breaths and let your eyes open.

CHAPTER VIII

TELLING THE TRUTH
TO YOURSELF AND OTHERS

"...one of the fundamental laws of life is this: whatsoever you hide goes on growing, and whatsoever you expose, if it is wrong it disappears, evaporates in the sun, and if it is right it is nourished".

Osho

In the previous chapters we have seen how identification with the mask of our personality and, more precisely, with the internal representations of ourselves and of the world around us make it impossible to live spontaneously and feel authentic.

We have also seen how the sense of uncertainty and loss of substantiality that we sometimes feel comes from the repetition of the original betrayal of our true nature that - in the name of survival, adaptation to the family ambience and the need to belong - happened in infancy. This betrayal, which continues to occur daily in thousands of different ways, is a deep wound in our psyche that we try to avoid at all costs and that, at the same time, will never leave us: On the contrary, it terrorizes us with the ever-present possibility of being found out, of being recognized as false, of being unmasked. A large part of our inner dialogue revolves around the maintenance of our personality's status quo, the prevention of any change that might threaten our external or internal self-image; summed up by our images of a world which we believe to be true, that gives us a special and distinct sense of identity.

We have also seen how remembering oneself means putting that sense of identity and one's personal history under scrutiny, beginning with the recognition that what we believe to be a "true" story is just an interpretation. We created this interpretation little by little over time and, with a sort of self-hypnosis, it has now become "the truth". We have seen how this identification manifests itself in life through some fundamental distortions that help to perpetuate and reinforce our false identity. I have called the unconscious participation to this false script the "contract of mediocrity".

I also said that an understanding of the relativity of truth as practiced daily can help us immensely in not creating conflicts and in resolving those that exist. On the one hand, the recognition of the relativity of our experience and the interpretation that we give weakens the structure of the personality because our identification with opinions, judgments and prejudices that are part of it diminishes. On the other hand we become more flexible and open and so, also more capable of responding to the mental, physical and emotional challenges that we meet. Our limits become less rigid and every part of our body responds appropriately and efficiently. In general, after an initial phase of disorientation, a weaker attachment to the structure means a stronger connection with the present and our True Nature: we become more present, stronger and more open to the natural splendor of Being. We find ourselves in that dynamic state you have probably sometimes been aware of: "feeling yourself flow", where everything seems to happen magically and without effort; without doubts or resistance and with simplicity and natural efficiency.

I then introduced the notion of "radical compassion", describing it to be like a motorway heading towards, and based essentially on, creative action and practical and real awareness of the fact that we are co-creators of the reality of our every moment. Finally I offered some techniques which, in my opinion, are very effective in helping us to dissolve our attachment to false identity and to support us in the pursuit of our true identity; that which we call the authentic Self.

Where am I?
The thread that connects all our understandings and the techniques

of attention/meditation and inquiry is that intertwining with our will and commitment to tell ourselves the truth about ourselves. We look at ourselves, we sense ourselves, we recognize our defenses and resistance, we observe the pattern of our behaviors and recognize their design, we are alert and so we are sensitive to attacks by the judge and the reactivity that derives from them, we sense our fear and anger, our self-judgments and our vulnerability: we have chosen to be ourselves and to embrace everything that we are. From a distance we also recognize "where" we are, not in relation to outside but "where" we are inside, in the intimacy of our inwardness. In recognition and in the acceptance of this "where" there is relaxation, there is the self-expression of the natural flow of Being and, often with great surprise, we begin to perceive, detect, the uniqueness of this manifestation of Being that which we call ME.

On this point Almaas says:

"This process of locating yourself is a profoundly personal one, a subtle and sensitive unfolding of inner awareness that does not use obvious external signposts to tell you where you are at any given time. It requires discipline and patience, gentleness and attunement, because the only one who can know where your consciousness is is you. To truly be where you are requires a capacity for listening, a willingness to be open, and a curiosity about your own experience that most likely few people have ever shown toward you" [13]

What a wonderful step, that of telling ourselves the truth, of sensing our readiness and being naked and transparent in front of our own eyes!

What freedom not having to lie to ourselves! And what peace we begin to feel when we don't struggle to hide who we are and what we feel from ourselves anymore, when we don't worry about denying our own intuition, when we don't have to defend what, deep down, we know to be false. And how much energy comes back to us! This process of reawakening to ourselves is also a process of recognition of the basic ground on which we stand. The "where" that we recognize is more than the place of our presence in time and space, it is a where that sinks and expands into eternity; when we sense where we are we begin to perceive that, in the continual change and flow of reality, there is a where that doesn't become different, doesn't move, doesn't change and that this where coincides with a sensation that we know well, very intimately, that of "me" who is always present during change: "me" was the "where" of the presence of baby and then the child and then the adolescent and into adulthood and now.

The next step: I expose myself

But all this, all this intimacy with ourselves and the truth that reveals itself to us, what use is it if it's not shared?: If it doesn't flower in relating and connecting with others?: If it doesn't also unite us with life on the outside?: If it doesn't change our way of speaking, loving, working, of listening, of sharing?

It is at this point that another step becomes almost inevitable and I say almost because it can be avoided, but it would be a real pity. This step involves learning to tell the truth about ourselves to others. Show yourself, let yourself be seen, be present and transparent with others, don't hide yourself, or, at least let's do our best to open ourselves up to the people around us, or at least to those that we love, so as to begin. Exposing ourselves to others is difficult as we have to face a very profound fear: what will people think of us? We have been hiding for so long, putting up a mask... since children, to please mum and dad, teachers, friends. It's not easy to show our original face.

"A trembling arises: will people like it? Will people accept you? Will people still love you, respect you? Who knows? – Because they have loved your mask, they have respected your character, they have glorified your garments. Now the fear arises: "If I suddenly become naked are they still going to love me, respect me, appreciate me, or will they all escape away from me? They may turn their backs, I may be left alone". Hence people go

on pretending. Out of fear is the pretension, out of fear arises all pseudoness. One needs to be fearless to be authentic".[14]

To tell myself the truth is THE fundamental step without which nothing else is possible. In recognizing and accepting the truth of my experience of the moment with all its ingredients and nuances, not only do I begin to re-member myself, but it becomes clear in what ways I create separation inside myself and with the world: What my defenses and beliefs are regarding external reality, how they are kept rigid, how I create a particular description of reality over and over again and how this description influences all my relationships. When I explore and begin to accept the rejected and condemned part of myself, my "shadow", I can also begin to see how this shadow, despite a continual struggle to hide it, is projected on the world in which I live and with which I interact. Entering into an intimate relationship with myself, I inevitably find myself confronting the ways in which my mask relates to other masks in a continuous game of make believe that can barely hide the fear that is behind. A natural need to share the recognition of a deeper Self, more real, also emerges resulting from my capacity to tell myself the truth about myself. I want to see, I want to know, I need to find out what will happen if I am truly myself; the natural tendency of BEING is towards expansion and manifestation. We recognize that inside there is an innate evolutionary urge, a vital force which conditioning has tried to contain; we recognize it costs us, and there has been a cost, an enormous effort to maintain our mask and pretend to be different to what we really are.

Conscious evolution

Often at this point we find ourselves feeling two forces that pull us in opposite directions: one of contraction, fed by fear and the past, which pulls us towards hiding ourselves, and another, fed by the evolutionary instinct for truth, that stretches out towards participation and the "risk" of being ourselves. In some ways we find ourselves reliving, this time in a conscious way, an inner situation very similar to the period of the "great betrayal". But now we have the opportunity to act in a completely different a way. If it's true that since childhood the approval of others, above all our parents, was a question of life and death and that therefore we didn't have much alternative to adapting to our environment renouncing essential parts of ourselves, now, as adults, we are in a very different situation (even though with very similar fears). Now, as adults, we can choose to support our true nature and to verify whether it is true that it's not acceptable to be ourselves and whether it is true that others will attack us or run away. We have the opportunity to really verify our capacity to live the truth we are discovering inside ourselves and to share it with the world around us. We have the opportunity to look fear in the face and to observe whether our fears are founded and real or whether they are just shadows from the past. We have the opportunity to stand up and assert our longing for authenticity and completeness.

In sharing the truth of our inner experience there are enormous implications and our personal growth and evolution is vastly accelerated. As human beings we are unique and complete in ourselves and at the same time we are related to everything that surrounds us. We are the drop and we are also the ocean. We don't exist in a separate way to everything else: every breath is an act of fusion with the universe where we give and receive, every glance, every movement, every sound, every touch. Relating to others, participating in the busy, lively manifestation of every moment as a part and creator of the river of existence is the fundamental expression of who we are and, until we are no longer in our bodies (and perhaps even after), it is inevitable. When we express the truth of what we are with our words and with our actions moment after moment, when we consciously and courageously share this life and reveal ourselves, the process of integration and of discovery of who we really are takes a quantum leap. Showing ourselves means strengthening ourselves, taking responsibility, affirming who we are in our own eyes and to others. We hear ourselves telling someone else about things we have long hid from ourselves, the thoughts become words, the interior sounds of truth are externalized, communicated, shared, and the words become action. And in the action of sharing ourselves, laying ourselves bare, our personal power once again returns and the fear of being ourselves, little by little, abandons our organism.

Telling the truth about ourselves to others not only liberates and integrates, it also creates a profound sense of dignity, a sense of the glory of our humanness and of our alignment with earth and sky, with gravity and grace.

We free ourselves from the need to justify and explain ourselves, we don't need find evidence of our value based on the past or the opinions of others, and this inner reflection, this harmony with our presence in the moment, is the opening through which we can gain direct experience of who we really are.

Inquiry

The first step in beginning to practice exposing yourself consists of looking inside yourself and working out who you can begin to practice with. The response, the one you're sure of, the one you can trust, won't come from your head, but from your heart or belly. It is there that we tremble with fear at the prospect of exposing ourselves and it is there we can find clues as to how, when and with whom we do it. At the same time, to prepare yourselves, you can explore a little:

a. Explore what happens to you when you think about sharing your most intimate experiences with others. First of all, observe the reactions in your body, whether there are contractions, whether you have the sensation that parts of your body almost "disappear" or, on the contrary, become as heavy as lead, whether these tensions encompass a "no" and what type of "no" it is, no, I can't do it, it's too much; no, it's dangerous; no, it's not worth it; no, no-one would be interested; no, it's not a good thing; no, I have nothing interesting to say; no, I'm better off on my own....and so on. Then begin to observe the emotions you feel: Rage? Fear? Resentment? Frustration? Distrust? Timidity? Resignation? Excitement? Observe whether you are under attack by your inner judge and, if so (and most probably you are), what your inner judge is saying and what the judgments of you and other people are. Take 10 minutes to do this first exploration and then jot down what seems to be, for you, the most essential points. Remember, it is also normal to have every sort of physical and emotional reaction just at the idea of opening up and telling the truth to someone. Don't let the superego beat you up!

b. Explore the reaction you had with your parents as a youngster when you found yourself having to/wanting to communicate with them about what was true for you: How did you feel? And how did they generally respond? Did you feel like you were listened to? Were they interested in what you said? Was there space for communication? Did they try and talk you round and make you change your mind? If possible go back to a real situation in which you have quite a clear memory and plunge into it: feel what physical sensations, emotions, and thoughts you are experiencing. Observe whether you can identify a particular dynamic that repeats itself in a specific way and note what you feel now in identifying that dynamic. Can you see if and how these ways are present today in your communication, or the lack of communication, with others? Take notes.

And finally...

c. Choose an intimate friend who you trust and with whom you are already inclined to confide in and share the results and the experience of the two previous explorations.

[13] Almaas A.H., The Unfolding Now, p.224
[14] Osho, The Guest, chap. 8

CHAPTER IX

IN SEARCH OF 'AUTHENTICITY':
INTENTION AND OPENNESS

"A path without a heart is never enjoyable. On the other hand, a path with heart is easy — it does not make a warrior work at liking it; it makes for a joyful journey; as long as a man follows it, he is one with it."
Don Juan Matus

When we live in ignorance of our true nature, we live under the illusion of existing as a separate identity, an entity, an object of our own consciousness and of other people's, a "thing" that we call me that, like an island surrounded by the sea, not only has boundaries and definition, but is also divided physically, mentally and spiritually from others and from the entire world. The most painful effect of the great betrayal is that it has created a fundamental division between matter and spirit, between body and soul in us. It has divided what I truly am from what I believe myself to be and present to the world in everyday life, it has separated my desire for material wealth and my longing for the luminosity of Being, it has separated my analytical and discriminating intelligence from my intuition, it has divided physical desires from spiritual pleasure and it has divided each one of us from the other. To live in an unconscious way and with the effects of the great betrayal is like living in a post atomic world, made up of failure and tattered dreams, made up of conflict and division, made up of remorse and things unsaid, of failed relationships, faded or never developed, made up of unlived passions, of unfulfilled needs, of fantasies that never bloomed, of tension and stress and, above all, made up of the subtle and constant sensation of not being in the right place and fully yourself.

The reality of daily life in which we live is, in most cases and most of the time, that of survival and, even if this is an inevitable necessity, it can't give us lasting satisfaction or a sense of complete happiness.

If the spirit doesn't permeate through all aspects of our lives on a permanent basis, there will always be a sense of loss, of inadequacy and remorse for the lost opportunity; of accidentally passing through this life almost as if in a dream.

If we don't stop considering ourselves and treating ourselves like things, bounded and limited, we miss out on the fundamental purpose of our existence which is to express the uniqueness of our souls.

We are the senses of the Universe and through each one of us the Cosmos manifests itself, recognizing itself and singing its song of transformation and evolution. Recognizing our spiritual nature and integrating this realization in our every day life means then to recognize and consciously express this individual and collective purpose.

Intention

Two fundamental elements guide and sustain us in the pursuit or better, rediscovery, of our authenticity: one - intention - that regards our will, the other - openness - which regards love.

Intention is the convergence and the unification in the present moment of attention, awareness and energy.

The desire to free myself from my false identity will not get me anywhere as long as it remains only a desire, however profound and impassioned. Desiring freedom can be a wonderful feeling but it is useless if it is not transformed into commitment and action. In fact, only that commitment and that action will take us away from our identification with being a victim of existence and of other people, and with the narcissist reactivity of the child that so often we become. If I want to be myself and realize my true potential I need to commit myself to transforming my desire for freedom into action and give priority in my life to this responsibility and this vision. This is a resolve, as necessary as it is fundamental, that isn't made only at the beginning but is also renewed during the journey, more and more times. It is then that the love for the truth becomes the light that illuminates our life and guides us in our most difficult times. Little by little this love for truth takes the place of fear for survival.

The intention of knowing the truth of a situation that I am living manifests itself as living curiosity, willingness and a commitment to being present with myself and everything that is occurring, alert, with profound interest and absorption. It is more than simply wanting the truth, it is also a determination to do everything that's necessary and possible: there is power, there is passion, there is tenacity, there is also flexibility and resilience. These last two qualities in particular are those that enable us to adapt to constant change without losing sight of our goal.

To sustain my intention of knowing myself I need to keep refocusing my attention on myself: my body and its sensations, the emotions I feel, changes of mood, thoughts and sentiments and to observe how they change and what effects they have on me.

Learning, with practice, to refocus my attention from the object of my experience (for example the line I am reading) to the experiencer (the perception of myself while reading) shifts the center of the same experience from outside to inside. Instead of focusing on what is happening outside I am focused on how I experience and my own awareness of it. This is what Osho calls "a turn of one hundred and eighty degrees": my attention turns to the inside. Every time we go through this turn not only does our attention move from the object to the subject of the experience, but also our awareness has a different focus and with this shift of awareness also our energy begins to flow towards the center instead of outwards. Our obsessive preoccupation with external objects is, in fact, probably the primary cause of our stress and lack of energy.

Openness

Openness is the receptive side of inquiry. It is the readiness to embrace every part of my experience and myself and let it be. Opening is saying yes to what happens inside and outside of me, in the awareness that every judgment, every prejudice, every resistance, every valuation, every rejection and attempt to change what I encounter, is the shadow of the past that protects itself trying to manipulate the present. It is the attempt by our superego (inner judge) to reaffirm its control on the functioning of the personality. To be open to myself and to the experience means then, to turn my attention to *sensing* myself rather than *thinking* about myself, to open all my senses and accept the information they give me NOW rather than looking for concepts in the past, ideas and immediate definitions. **I learn to remain open to myself and to the present experience and in that way I develop the capacity to encompass fragments of understanding, waiting for the whole design to reveal itself.** Instead of manipulating myself and my experience folding it all up to make it fit in the categories and priorities of my mind, I let the significance and understanding emerge from the present moment while keeping my attention sharp and observing its unfolding and the movement of my reactions. I overcome the compulsive need to find immediate answers in order to alleviate my fear of the unknown and of failure and I learn to wait, keeping alive my curiosity, vitality, intelligence.

Knowing oneself has little to do with finding answers and a lot to do with learning to ask questions. The more precise and real the questions are, the more the answers will emerge like revelations of the present moment and the result of our intention and of our openness. Feeling the presence of intention and openness in our bodies is delightfully exciting: it's like the atoms of our cells move more rapidly while potential energy becomes dynamic and what was once a possibility is now transformed into reality. It is a state of alert resulting from the accompanying activation of all our physical and spiritual senses: the inner senses. It is a sensation as hidden as it is strangely familiar, forgotten since childhood, of excitement for potential discovery, of amazement facing the rich complexity of the universe that we are and that surrounds us, of the delicate intricacy of every moment. We are hunters of ourselves and of the truth of our being and of our feelings. It is like being a cat that lies down in front of a hole waiting for a mouse, relaxed, sure of its own capacity, alert, with all its senses open and ready to strike. And you are the cat and also the mouse and with your intention and your openness disentangle the weave of reality behind the mask, behind the conditioning, behind falseness and old notions, with patient intensity to return home and know yourself directly, immediately, without filters or concepts.

The promise that is impossible to keep.
In the journey that takes us from identification with the false self of the personality to awareness of our True Nature and of the unique expression of our authentic Self, there is an obstacle that I wouldn't really know how to define because of the profoundness with which it is inscribed in our cells and hidden from our consciousness: we have made a promise.

At a certain point in our childhood we made a promise swearing to ourselves that we would never become like her (Mum) or him (Dad). Or we made a promise to the contrary, that we would be able to be like him or her, or we promised to be like one of them but not the other. A promise that comes from natural love, immeasurable and primordial, of a child for his parents.

Whatever this promise may be, the great majority of us made this promise, and in almost every case, it is forgotten. Nevertheless if you look carefully at your life, your relationship with your parents, your relationships with other people that you love, your impression of yourself as the years go by, perhaps you can see how this promise was not only made, but how it still affects your relationship with yourself, with others and the way you perceive the world.

This contract with ourselves and our parents, which is profound and primitive, securely hidden in our unconscious, influences our lives limiting them in unimaginable ways. Without even realizing, we spend a huge amount of physical and emotional energy day after day to sustain that promise we made to ourselves, even after having cancelled it from our conscious mind, even when we have supposedly separated from our parents and live independent lives, and even when our parents are dead.

If you decide to explore your past, and above all your heart, to find that promise, you need to be well aware that that promise is most probably a cornerstone of the structure of your personality and that it has been there for a major part of your life. And the consequences of letting go of that promise are very profound as they will impact on all the ways of perceiving yourself and the world around you. Letting go that promise means letting go of a specific image of ourselves as children in relation to specific images of our parents as adults and as our first objects of love and adoration. It means accepting the risk of growing up and of the radical transformation of ties that we have with our past and with our mums and dads. It means freeing an enormous amount of energy that is currently blocked inside that promise and having that energy available for ourselves. It also means liberating our parents from the images that we unconsciously continue to project of them and opening up the real possibility of meeting them as human beings, in their beauty and splendor and with their limitations.

When we become conscious of the contract, powerful forces long repressed are liberated in our body, in our emotions and in our minds. Memories return, images, events long forgotten, sensory impressions, essential pieces of our childhood experiences and our great natural love for them - mother and father - and the happiness, the passions, the rush and the caresses, the delusions and the refusals, the warmth and the solitude, and all the events that have determined the necessity for this contract. This process is unpredictable in its length and intensity, and is an integral part of the cathartic process of liberation of our own unconscious from the weight of the past.

In this phase two things are essential:

1. To have a guide capable of supporting us, whether a therapist, a teacher or a spiritual master.

2. To begin and to maintain over time a regular practice of inquiry and of meditation.

The presence of a therapist/teacher to support us during the process of dismantling the personality and false identity, principally through his function as the mirror of our process and his capacity to offer a holding environment in which we feel safe when facing moments of crisis.

The practice of inquiry is the key that opens the door of our unconscious, it activates our awareness and remembrance, guides the process of reconnection with ourselves fuelled by our love for the truth and it responds to our curiosity and passion.

Meditation is the art of creating an inner space where it is possible to become aware of ourselves, and in its quality of returning to the source of Being, it is also the opening of a space of tranquility and serenity that enables our creativity to manifest itself and from there to return to the world with new inspiration.

The technique that follows is simply an initial taste in our search for the promise we made. If you feel that it concerns you, then begin to use it regularly.

The technique.

Find a quiet place where there's no distraction and take all the time you need.

The technique begins with an exploration of your emotions, at this moment, while remembering your parents. Remembering them one by one is more efficient in that your emotions are clearly directed at the parent you are recalling. Feel the sensations in your body, whether there is tension and where, whether you feel happiness through these memories and cheerfulness, or a heaviness and sense of anxiety, or something else. Let everything be okay, don't manipulate your experience, feel whether you are pulled towards your parent or pushed away, whether you want to go closer or distance yourself, whether there is warmth or coldness... open yourself fully to the experience, NOW. Let memories of childhood come afloat in a spontaneous way and, while noting your sensations, ask yourself if you have ever made a promise like the one described previously. The related sensations of having done so can be very subtle and vague or there may be a very precise memory, whatever the situation try to be as aware as possible to the details of your memories, of your images and of what you feel at this moment. If and when you have the opportunity, explore what the consequences have been of this promise in your life up until now.

In this same session or in a following session you can decide to let this promise go if that is what you want and to do it you only have to decide internally that it is not necessary to keep it anymore.

Proceed in the same way with the other parent or whoever else you have made promises to in the past.

CHAPTER X

THE PARADOX OF SELF

"There are more things in heaven and earth, Horatio,
Than are dreamt of in your philosophy".
William Shakespeare

It is fascinating that modern science is constantly finding more "proof" of the fundamental unity of the universe and of its non-separation: As a matter of fact, every thing, including ourselves, is connected and in communication with everything else. By different routes and in different ways quantum physics, neuroscience, biochemistry, astronomy and many other sciences, all come to agree about the paradoxical nature of the universe. Multiple infinite synchronous realities, time and non-time, matter and anti-matter, black holes, the principle of uncertainty by Heisenberg, the principle of observation, the theory of strings, the analysis of the sub-atomic structure of the human body: scores of research "prove" that reality is completely different to what we perceive with our senses and that the world we see and we believe to be true is just a description sustained and kept going by an internal programme conditioned by the past and by conditioned senses: That we are not lost and segregated little islands, victims of something much greater than ourselves, but an essential part and co-creators of reality. We are pure consciousness, the incarnate manifestation of the divine. Perhaps one day science "will prove" that underneath the personality, there is a mysterious universe, AN OCEAN OF POTENTIALITY, and that that is our true nature.

But that "proof" (when and if it happens) will still be another something that will be offered to us externally and, however intriguing, it will still be an idea, a concept, and not our direct and incontestable experience; existential and not mental. External proof cannot quench our thirst for the truth, only direct experience can give us what it is we are looking for. Only DIRECT AND IMMEDIATE UNDERSTANDING of our nature, and the nature of the reality in which we live, will satisfy the longing of our soul, melt survival-fear, open the doors to the eternal, erase the tension of separation and illuminate the present moment with joyous surprise and innocent wonder.

Ah! Behind the mask, the mystery

The greatest surprise that greets us when we lift the veil of the personality in search of our authentic Self, is that the mystery of one's self, instead of disappearing, becomes much more vast and profound. When the mask of false identity is raised, the false concepts that cover reality begin to dissolve and reality starts to show itself. We abandon our obsessive need for answers that give us false certainty and we begin to look with respect and reverence at the continuous transformation of reality and of ourselves within it.

The mask becomes visible, often clear and evident: when we look carefully at ourselves and at our behavior it's not difficult to recognize how the structure of the personality, with its attachment to the past, its limitations, repetitiveness, convictions, opinions, points of view and absolute certainty is, in its entirety, just a defense against the immensity and the mystery of Being and of Becoming. In fact, when the personality starts to lose consistency and become more fluid, what we begin to glimpse is not a territory made of certainty, definitions and irrefutable concepts, on the contrary, the reality that presents itself has a quality that we can truly know only if we go beyond the limits of mental and dualistic reasoning, and of linear logic.

At the same time something also happens, that was well recognized by ancient religions, and that is our perception of reality is inverted:

"...when our consciousness is dim and our attention is on the external world we see this body and everything that exists as substantial and something like spirit as insubstantial. But when we begin to awaken into the state of enlightenment, inversion takes place. So what is substantial before begins to become more and more insubstantial and what appears to be insubstantial becomes more and more substantial".[15]

In simply becoming aware of how what we considered to be a solid and certain reality is just a description and that the identity to which we are accustomed is just a convention, the doors that lead to perception of the Spirit are opened.

There are many qualities of the authentic self, all surprising and fascinating, and even more ways in which each one of us manifest them in absolute uniqueness.

In part IV of this book we will meet some of them through the essays of friends who I asked to write about their experience, or one of their experiences, of the true Self.

Here I want to now tackle the central quality of Self, that which I believe to be the most important, and namely its paradoxical nature, which in the moment in which we discover it, arrives at the same time completely unexpectedly and with absolute familiarity.

I will approach this combining understanding and experience and guide you through processes of mental understanding and exercises of experiential recognition, combining the two for all of the initial phase and then letting the mind go, towards the end, when we find ourselves at the threshold of direct experience of the Self.

To do this, I will begin any moment now to guide you through a process of inner exploration through the question "Who am I?" which is, without doubt, one of the quickest and efficient ways to gain direct experience of yourself. This inquiry dates back thousands of years and is central to the recognition of our True Nature, and today, it is practiced in different ways by various schools of mysticism. It is also a fundamental element of my spiritual teaching above all in a retreat called Satori, a Japanese word which means "lamp of illumination" and refers to the moment in which the seeker experiences his own nature, or as Zen would say, meets his "original face".

In the previous chapters you received various spiritual "tools" that can help your exploration and, in particular, those of intention and opening, and if they're not completely clear, please re-read chapter IX before going on.

Choice-less awareness

Awareness without choice is the last thing you need in the journey. In my experience, these three words are the best definition or better, the actual soul of meditation: "awareness without choice" indicates the possibility of realizing the ultimate nature of reality, letting go whatever preferences we have with regards to our experience of the moment. It means recognizing what is going on around us as well as internally without attaching ourselves to or rejecting what happens, but rather being simply like a mirror that reflects what it is facing us in a neutral, exact way, unbiased. When we are in such a situation it is like watching a film that's going on both in front of our eyes and inside us and we are the spectators: inquisitive, participating, but always aware of being observers of the show.

The process that I describe in the following pages is an incomparable adventure, a journey of awakening, sometimes very demanding in which it is easy to lose yourself, and in which I too have lost myself many times. But in the same way that we lose ourselves, we find ourselves, and something in the meantime will be absorbed and metabolized, and we will be closer to our center. This coming back home could last hours, days, months or years, but what is certain is it is worth it.

Being is not being, not being is being.

"Then, due to the suffering that arises out of being lost, one finds the unconditioned as oneself"[16]

Step 1.
At least 20 minutes

Begin by closing your eyes and sit down comfortably and with your back straight. Take a few minutes to settle inside yourself, sense your body and the position it has assumed, sense your breathing as air flows in and out, raising your chest and, perhaps moving your belly. Let your senses be open and allow all your sensory impressions present in this moment: don't avoid anything, don't attach yourself to anything, don't reject anything, let everything be exactly as it is. When you feel that you are settled and that your attention is free to move without attaching itself to anything, then begin to ask yourself: who am I? Let the answers come by themselves and observe how you feel in relation to these replies or to the absence of them.

When we enter into ourselves to do inquiry with the most existential of questions, "Who am I?", **initially we will encounter the most superficial layers of the personality**; those that define our sense of identity: our beliefs, opinions, concepts, memories that are part of our personal history and the way in which we define ourselves in everyday life. We have a name, a sex, a nationality, a skin color, a religion, a job, a role, and so on: so we are Henry or Lynn or Francesca, we are men or women, Italian, American, Korean, South African, black, yellow, white, we are Muslim, Buddhist, Christian, office or factory workers, artists, teachers, fathers, mothers, sisters. In conclusion we have various labels that define our identity in the world and with which we identify ourselves.

Looking carefully (and if we are willing to tell ourselves the truth about ourselves) sooner or later we will recognize that all these things qualify our story and our function but they don't get anywhere near giving us a satisfactory answer to our question. In fact, I am more than my name; it's just a nameplate, I amount to more than my nationality; it's just an indication of where I was born. I am more than my religion, the one I received from my family or chose later in years, I am more than my sex; it's a productive role as well as a specific psychological trait, and I am certainly more than

97

my job, that represents what I DO, not what I AM. These definitions, then, don't satisfy my question in any way, but only identify my personality in its social context. At the same time it is clear that **inside somewhere there is a ME to whom all these definitions refer and there is a ME that is conscious of defining myself in these ways**. Look how Osho describes this process and this understanding:

"Meditation is unlearning, unlearning is meditation. What in fact do you do when you meditate? You simply unlearn the mind; by and by you drop the layers and layers of mind. You are like an onion, you go on peeling yourself: one layer – the most superficial – is thrown, another layer comes up, you throw that, you drop that also, another comes up – and it goes on and on"…"Meditation is unlearning. Peel your onion. It is difficult because you have become identified with the onion, you think these layers are you. So to peel them is difficult, it is painful also because it's not just like throwing your clothes, it is rather peeling your skin. You have become too attached to it. But once you know, once you drop one layer you feel freshness arising. You become new. Then courage increases, then hope, then you feel more confident; then you can peel another layer. The more you peel the more silent, the happier, the more blissful you become. Now you are on the right track".[17]

Step 2.
Twenty minutes or more.
Once again, with your eyes closed, take time to feel your body and reconnect yourself with the present moment. Feel, listen, watch everything that appears in your consciousness and don't attempt to control or change what is, here/now. **Go back to the question: Who am I?** Note whether it is different to hear yourself asking yourself this question, now that the most external layers, the ones that identify you in this world, show themselves exactly for what they are: just external images that serve to identify you in relation to others.

If you eliminate all the outer definitions/identifications and, moving your attention inside, you will get closer to yourself then you can begin to ask yourself: am I these body's sensations, am I the emotions I feel and the thoughts that I have? Am I my body? Am I my feelings? Am I my mind? Here the search gets more interesting and the identification more profound. Also here, if you look carefully and inquisitively, you will note that all these things change continually: every moment, new sensations, new emotions, new thoughts, at the speed of light: A continuous movement, an incessant flow, like rush hour traffic.

But is it really like this? Feel, listen, observe and focus your attention. You will then see no, it's not like this, it's just an impression that disappears all of a sudden when you are completely present and absorbed in the here/now. There are spaces between your thoughts, between your emotions, between your sensations and between them: it's not a continuous sequence, in the traffic there are pauses and moments of silence.

You may realize then that all the phenomena you are conscious of appear in an inner space. In this space, objects with various form and consistency come and go, appear and disappear like clouds in the sky and waves on the ocean's crest or bubbles of air in fizzy wine. Some of these phenomena are material objects: they are daily objects that we take for granted, that surround us, and that we use to live. Others are immaterial objects that we experience "internally" in the form of thoughts, emotions and sensations. Despite being immaterial they are, however, objects in your consciousness and they also come and go and change continually. This or that thought, happiness, anger, greed, a headache or a smile, it is the "I" that experiences all this. And while all these things change in a continual flow of events, the "I" continues to be the one that has experience and is conscious of it. It's clear then that "I" is the "subject" of the experience and that, as subject, conscious of "objects" in the experience.

The realization of this simple reality: the existential relationship between "I" that experiences and various objects that are experienced is the basis of the next step, in which we completely move our attention away from the "things" which we experience (the WHATS) to concentrate entirely on "WHO" has the experience. Let's remember, in fact, that our original question, the heart of our exploration, is not **"What am I?"** but **"Who am I". Who is conscious? Who experiences?**

Pause for a moment at this point. Perhaps this process is too quick and seemingly complex. Let's try and practice now, as you read.

Sit down, if you're not already sat down, and rest your right hand on your knee. Feel the temperature of this hand, the pressure on your knee and whatever other sensations you are feeling, without paying attention to judgments and mental evaluation, stay present in your physical sensations. This is your sensory experience of your knee at this moment, and this experience is the object of your consciousness: you (subject) are conscious of your hand on your knee (object). But not only: You are also conscious of reading, thinking, evaluating what you're reading, of there being a book in front of you, that maybe poses questions, that maybe there is skepticism or excitement, understanding, perhaps you're conscious of the light around you, background noises or of your breathing, and so on. YOU ARE THE CENTER OF YOUR EXPERIENCE MOMENT BY MOMENT.

That's where we are, wouldn't you agree? We have arrived at the point of recognizing that "I" is the center from which all experiences depend: everything that happens is indeed experienced by YOU through your consciousness. To use a poetic image: you are the sun around which the events of existence rotate whether they are external and material, or internal and immaterial.

This realization is revolutionary in itself, and often not easy to accept, especially if our conditioning is based heavily on the conviction that our personal value depends on the approval of others. Here, in fact, a true and real inner Copernican revolution occurs: **I am the center of the universe and my consciousness is the fundamental ground on which all objects appear (including others who might define my value as a human being!)**

Step 3
As long as you need

At this point we can turn our attention completely to the subject of experience, "I", and let go of the objects, whatever they might be, material or immaterial.

This transition is the fundamental progression of self-inquiry because, perhaps for the first time, we will finally focus our attention directly on the Self and not indirectly, in a mediated way, through our continual relationship with different types of objects. Who am I? Who is this "I" that is conscious of everything that is happening around, one's body, thoughts, or moods and sentiments? **I am the subject of all experience...** and here the mind begins to have some difficulty following, because our minds only understand the language of duality and can't understand the existence of a subject without including an object at the same time.

To quote Osho once again:

"When I say, "Go inwards", that does not mean that you will find someone there waiting for you. On the contrary, the more you go inwards, the less and less you are an ego. You are, but the feeling of I-ness starts disappearing – for the simple reason that the I can exist only in reference to Thou. If the Thou is not present, the I starts melting. Outside you are confronted by many Thous, they keep your I alive. But inside, there is no Thou; hence, there can be no I. That does not mean that you are not. It simply means that you are in your purity –not in reference to somebody else, but just yourself, without any reference, in your absolute aloneness".[18]

This is also the classic transition in meditation where the observer's focus of contemplation is moved from the object of observation to the observer himself: **watching the watcher, witnessing the witness.**
Close your eyes and focus your attention as much as possible, and possibly exclusively, on the question "who am I?", abandon every effort to reply, abandon every "thing" that comes into your conscious and sense with all your might whether there is someone inside, whether you can find, catch a glimpse, detect someone. Feel,

observe, listen carefully, don't rush yourself. Is someone there? Can you find a you separate from you who are searching? Don't look with your mind, open up your senses as if you're a wild animal in the forest. Trust your intuition, your feelings, the instinctive vibrations of your senses, in your skin, in the keenness of your hearing. Finding yourself is not a mental process, it requires a profound alignment of all our faculties and a reawakening to our most primitive heritage, dormant memories, hidden, forgotten. Becoming centaurs, finding the animal in us, the cloud, the flower, the rock, and the opening to a possible, primordial, immense, unknown and potential future. Who am I? Who am I?

And you will NOT find anyone, for the very simple reason that there is no one. There is only presence, the sense of existing, empty space, silence... **and at the same time there is you, conscious of all that.** Here is the paradox: you don't exist as a thing, an entity, a somebody, and yet you are here, as a unique and original incarnation of the cosmic consciousness.

You are pure consciousness, unconditioned, uncontaminated, always present, reflecting every form that appears. You are the paradox, the being that isn't.

You are the inner space that is empty of objects and full of you, full of the presence that you are.

Stop. And note what happens inside when you read these words. Do they sound familiar? Is it true that when you go inside you don't find anyone? Don't you believe in what I am saying, go inside, find that subject without losing yourself in the objects and give yourself your own answer in a way that it is certain, unquestionable, your own direct experience ..... and let reality surprise you.
Here are some provisions for your journey:

Eckhart Tolle:
"That happened to me. I was just that close to suicide and then something else happened—a death of the sense of self that lived through identifications,

identifications with my story, things around me, the world. Something arose at that moment that was a sense of deep and intense stillness and aliveness, beingness. I later called it "presence." I realized that beyond words, that is who I am".[19]

And Osho:

"Who am I? My entire being was throbbing with this thirst. What a violent storm it was! Every breath quaked and trembled in it. "Who am I?" – like an arrow, the question pierced through everything and moved within. I remember – what an acute thirst it was! My very life had turned into thirst. Everything was burning. And like a flame of fire the question stood forth, "Who am I?" The surprise was that the intellect was completely silent. The incessant flow of thoughts had stopped. What had happened? The periphery was absolutely still. There were no thoughts, no conditionings of the past. Only I was there – and there was the question too. No, no – I myself was the question.

And then the explosion. In a moment, everything was transformed. The question had dropped. The answer had come from some unknown dimension. Truth is attained through a sudden explosion, not gradually. It cannot be compelled to appear. It comes. Emptiness is the solution, not words. Becoming answerless is the answer".[20]

And Avikal:

The Gardener has been weeding,
Turning the soil, moving rocks,
Opening narrow pathways,
Sending the rain to wash the dust
And the wind to spread the seeds,
Sending the birds to sit on the branches
And sing their love,
Sending the moon and the sun
To create shadows of silver and gold.
What did I do?
A small price it was to be paid:

I left behind the skin of my suffering and ignorance
And walked in naked,
Radiant with the light of Being.
Now I sit in the garden
And see him.[21]

[15] *Kimura Yasuhiko Genku, Working for Good, video interview by Jeff Klein for the magazine Flow, www.via-visioninaction.org*
[16] *Tolle Eckhart, Ripples on the Surface of Being, an interview by Andrew Cohen. What is Enlightenment magazine, September-December 2006*
[17] *Osho, Tao: The Three Treasures, Vol.3 Chapter 4*
[18] *Osho, The Golden Future, chapter 8*
[19] *Tolle Eckhart, Ripples on the Surface of Being, an interview by Andrew Cohen. What is Enlightenment magazine, September-December 2006*
[20] *Osho, Seeds of Wisdom, n.13*
[21] *Avikal E. Costantino, Traces, CD of poetry by Avikal and music by Murray Burns, Byron Bay, Australia 2002*

Part IV

STORIES OF TRUE SELF

Behind the fire of jealousy
By Rafia Morgan

In contemplating experiences of True Being I am drawn to a particular memory because it was a rather dramatic lesson in how a Being can arise out of any experience if we are simply able to stay present with our experience without judgment or interpretation. I have remembered this experience as living proof and a deep sense of inner resource that showed me that hell can truly be transformed into heaven. The agent of change in this situation was facing a very difficult inner demon—jealousy.

I had been together with my girl friend for close to four years. We had been under a lot of stress from external circumstances for over six months at the time and we had fallen into a space of not being able to feel close, understand each other or feel very connected. It seemed that no matter what we did or tried, we just couldn't return to the space of love that had carried us in the past and we couldn't move forward into something new that made us feel connected. It was frustrating, nerve-wracking and at times both very mental and emotional. Throughout this period of time we stayed together in a situation that involved very much traveling and external change and while all of that was happening it was as though a barrier had settled between us that we just couldn't dissolve or get through. At a certain point a night came when she didn't come home until very late and my worst fears were realized... she told me she was attracted to another man and wanted to spend some time with him. I was very upset and it looked like we would separate but before we could really look to see what was right for us to do we were suddenly forced to travel again and the issue of her relating to him was put to the side in the intensity of travel and practical arrangements.

About one month later we had settled and it seemed that things were starting to get calm. Then one morning I was told by one of the friends we were staying with that my girl friend had left to meet the man she had been attracted to and that the two of them were going to return together that night! I felt cast into hell in that moment—my heart was broken, my trust was shattered, I felt deeply betrayed and very angry, I felt humiliated in front of my friends as well as feeling rejected and exposed as an inadequate man. It was truly one of the worst and most traumatic moments of my life hearing that news. I felt my legs go weak and my head spin. I wanted to run but couldn't. I wanted to smash the furniture but didn't. After an hour or so and realizing that I was going to have to face them and the situation when they returned, I decided to go to my room and hide. Hiding was not the answer either as I was so restless I couldn't be still; my mind was playing horror show scenes and my body felt sick. Finally I decided to see what would happen if I would just lie down and go into the experience instead of react to it. I was drawn to my solar plexus area as there was so much anxiety and tension there. At first it was almost impossible to keep my focus there as my mind was dragging me out into its dramatic movie where I could feel sorry for myself. At one point though, I remember being able to ask myself the question: "what is this reaction really about?" I realized I had been suffering for months in some tension that no matter how hard I efforted or how much I shared with my girl friend simply did not go away. I had been compulsively trying to deal with the anxiety, to "solve" it, to make it go away. I was not really going deep into it but was reacting to it as it touched deeper wounds and fears that I was not ready to face. Seeing that, inquiring and committing myself to face my feelings in their entirety this time, I felt the first tiny stirring of relaxation which informed me I was on the right track. Over the next few hours, with some ups and downs, I faced this fear, this humiliation, betrayal and rage by simply experiencing the sensations that were in my body and by allowing pictures from my past and insights about my behavior to all pass by and through me. It was an experience of feeling like a rope that was wound very tight which was slowly unwinding and opening so that each strand became loose and flexible. I noticed that my mind started to relax and that my heart and the corners of my mouth were faintly smiling. I felt gratitude creeping in. I felt free and I was happy to be released from the situation that had been making me so miserable. When the moment came where I heard them outside my window I was able to jump to my feet, go outside and embrace them both without any feeling other than love. I remember it as one of the happiest moments of my life. I was also incredulous in some old corner of my mind but the experience was authentic and undeniable. I was laughing inside at the absurdity of my suffering and rejoicing in the freedom as I sincerely wished them well.

I recognized some hours later that this was a shift from the tightness of my personality to the truth of my being. I remember taking a walk that night on the beach and crying to the stars my thank you. There was not one thought of them being together and not one single worry about anything. I was profoundly Home. That experience has given me an inner blue print to my Being that I still refer to when something hits me in a way that triggers my personality with all of its conditions. I may still at times wallow in an emotional tide for awhile but then I remember to just be present with the experience and that Being itself is inviting me to remember a deeper truth....and this remembering is both the key back home and the greatest source of blessing I have known.

And every time I laugh about it

by Anna Zanardi

Every time life throws me a wake up-call with a new surprising event, and generally my obtuseness causes me to need quite strong kicks, I am stunned for an instant and then, with more or less compassion towards me being as I am, I find myself smiling for a moment, then laughing about it. Did I still believe I could decide how to satisfy some needs or desires, was I still thinking I could lead my life in an ordered way; socially correct? Was I still thinking I could let the present go and automatically head towards that abstract concept that is the future?

So, when I forget that extraordinary gift that is the present day; when I forget how much I can contribute to building, creating, giving to others, because I am concentrating a little too much on my ego, then existence takes over. And even if I don't always immediately appreciate its forms and ways, thanks to my awareness and presence I end up laughing at my carelessness.

Looking back again at the road that leads from my birth to today, once again I see a shapeless tangle; of fatigue, pain, loneliness and abandonment that becomes slowly slowly illuminated by sense and gratitude. I have met some extraordinary people, some who have loved me and some who have left me helpless when faced by danger or death, some who have given me a hand and some who have just pretended to, some who have treated me with love and some who have used violence, some who have respected me and some who have exploited my weaknesses, some who have recognized my value and appreciated me and others who have humiliated me and looked down on me, some who have "seen" me and others who have ignored me and still continue to look right through me.

I wouldn't know who to thank the most, because each time it is an opportunity to scratch away a piece of the mask, to unveil that cumbersome and cantankerous inner judge that we all know, but never well enough, and we always underestimate. Every gesture, every word, every happiness and every pain has made sense; shown its significance, and they have taught me that the only thing really worthwhile looking for in any situation is a splinter of authenticity; mine, his, hers, the others'. Eye to eye, hands stretched out and, if possible, your body relaxed and your mind switched off.

Making an effort won't help, I just let time pass by in the presence of my heart; I observe every emotion that comes from inside and I know how useful it can be to be forthcoming, firstly to myself and then those who want to share.

It's wonderful to see how when the knot disentangles, the road gets wider, people gather together and a collective force, much bigger than what we are individually, flows with strength and intelligence, in silence. Who knows where it will take us or bring us back to?

From There to Here
By Ganga Cording

A poet wrote:
IN THE EVENING
IF IT WERE RAIN
WE SHOULD SEEK SHELTER,
BUT THINKING, "IT IS ONLY MIST"
WE GO ON AND BECOME DRENCHED.

He is not talking about the rain outside, he is talking about your inside. Don't be afraid – get drenched in the mist, in the mystery. And when you come back, come back a totally different person. The one who has gone in should be left behind, and you should take a new face – your original face. Dropping the mask and bringing out your original face is the whole alchemy of meditation.
Osho, Buddha: *The Emptiness of the Heart*, Chapter #6

(Words in italics are exclamations of people describing the true self thrown in at random)

All the distinctions (mind, ego, personality, being, true self, inner, outer etc.) are good working hypotheses but they don't exist as entities. They are useful to lay out the map of the inner but just as each landscape is part of the same one world so are all these distinctions the expressions of the same one consciousness, the same true self.

"I am"

To find the true self one has to lose oneself. The true self refers to what we are born with, call it the being, me, soul, godliness. The part which requires the spring clean refers to the part called personality and ego. It contains the stuff we have acquired during a lifetime of learning, with a flood of habits, beliefs, ideas, and identifications. This has created a more or less tight frame of mind which we live our life with. Mostly there is no awareness of a frame, or the effort of carrying it around, or the illusion of mistaking it as reality. The good news is we are not any of it, we have only accumulated it on top of the true self and therefore we can let go of it. The word mind implies ambiguity. Often we hear one has to drop the mind in order to experience the true self and come to a state of no-mind. Then it looks as if the mind is the enemy which has to be eliminated. Yes it is true, mind is the root cause of all misery and yet it is not the enemy. Ramesh Balsekar makes a useful distinction between the thinking mind and the working mind. As I understand it the thinking mind is I-centered. It contains all the interpretations, judgments, the good and bad, the musts and must nots, the worries, and the habitual, compulsive ego-centered ways of dealing with reality. Then there is the working mind which is a simple mechanism dealing with the facticity of life, like remembering where the next grocery store is. Living with the thinking mind creates hell, living with the working mind makes life easy and living with no-mind is heaven. Moving into a state of no-mind doesn't mean to turn into a mindless zombie without a brain. It rather is being very alive and conscious in a state of surrender to what is, fully present in the here and now, no interpretation, no wanting any different, in a let go, one with existence. It is being- or existence oriented.

"Anal hak", I am truth

The direct experience of the true self is not an experience in fact and not a state either. It is the very existence of each one of us, the foundation of all. All experiences are part of time, they come and go. The true self doesn't come and go, it is always here; only the mental recognition of it comes and goes. But language is very limited and doesn't seem to provide a better expression. And there is the paradox that one cannot write about the experience of the true self either, one can only experience it directly. It's like trying to describe the taste of an apple. Biting into it is easy. One knows immediately how the texture is how it tastes. It is a direct experience, it's either mmmh! or brrh! It is immediate, right in the moment, it's total. There is no doubt or insecurity; there is nothing in between (me and the experience). It simply is, alive in the present. But the moment I try to describe how this taste was (description will always be somewhat after the experience) the problem starts. When I say sweet, is it sweet for you also or perhaps you find it sour? With description one enters the jungle of definitions, terminologies, concepts, different languages and private connotations.

"Ah This!"
The first experiences of the true self are usually glimpses and often happen by accident; in nature watching the splendor of a sunset, swimming in the ocean, being in love, or in a near to death experience. Even in these momentary fleeting experiences of the true self all the ingredients of the true self are already present: timelessness, relaxation, restfulness, divineness, godliness, innocence, aliveness, freedom, spaciousness, expansion, peacefulness, ease, love, something bigger than me, joy, beauty, silence. There is the sense of 'yes that is how it is meant to be', of being at home, as many participants in the Awareness-Intensive and Satori retreats have described it. There is also a faint remembrance of something lost long ago. This recognition creates a longing to have more of it, to remember fully, and to gain access in a more conscious way. For many this is a turning point in their life and the beginning of taking up the practice of meditation.

"I am freedom"
These first glimpses can be like seeing a light in the dark for the first time. It is breathtaking, alerting and perhaps even blinding. Then the eyes get accustomed and looking becomes easier. When more of these glimpses happen the experience is more of an outlook into the landscape of the inner, and less of a dazzling event. One is

looking at the whole through a hole. A longing to find out 'what is this?' and 'who am I?' is growing; a much needed fuel on the road to find oneself. A better expression is to rediscover oneself, to be the consciousness we are.

"This, this a thousand times this"
To be the true self one has to let go of all that is known as me, which can be very scary and challenging. Worse! One is usually not done with going through this mind shattering experience once only, it happens over and over again as these frames of mind become obvious in the direct experience of the true self and as the inner horizon opens more and more. It's like a frame in the frame in the frame, each more spacious as the one before but a frame still. To set out to become an individual in all its glory, undivided and strong, settling in ones true self is not easy but the only thing really satisfying in life. No 'other oriented' gratification, fame, success, riches can compete with the simple resting in ones true self.

"I am consciousness"
Coming out of the confinement of the mind and dissolving as I, me, ego, persona into the 'big mind', It, god, All, or whatever you call it, is what we most long for and are most afraid of at the same time. Going in can be in the beginning like dying or having one foot on the accelerator while the other is on the brake. The heart is longing to go home and the mind is pulling all tricks to hold the reins, very creative indeed! This is when determination and inner discipline are needed. 'Holding the nose ring tight?' to use a phrase from the story of the ten Zen bulls. Inner discipline is born out of the understanding that one needs to follow ones own inner nose and should not to be confused with discipline imposed from the outside. Outer discipline is the fruition of ideas, ideals and duty. Inner discipline is the expression of a high sensitivity to oneself, it is love for the true self.

"I am love"

Another aspect of the true self is that one cannot claim ownership or brag about to have found it. It's not something one can accomplish. It is given, it is life itself. Yes one is the true self but there is nobody to claim. The experience of I am is an existential fact and everybody's birthright. It should be celebrated and shouted from the rooftops but it it's not me or you who created it. Moments of no-mind appear sudden and are a happening. There is nothing one can do to make them happen. They are a gift from existence. And they don't make one enlightened either. To me it only makes sense to speak of enlightenment when the experience of no-mind is coming through in one's every action. One lives and acts moment to moment from no-mind. Though rooted in the moment it is not a momentary affair.

"Aham Brahasmi "– I am God

 As long as the old mind is there these moments of no-mind will be buried soon enough. Therefore the old mind has to be trained to overcome the 'inertia of habits' as Osho called it; not unlike the reframing in NLP (Neo Linguistic Programming). Once the mind is convinced that living in accordance with ones being and resting in ones true nature is the better way it will start to cooperate and relax. It lets go of the society and past oriented moralistic language and becomes willing to learn a new, more colorful language, the language of the inner. This language is the expression of the being and the truth of the moment. It comes straight from the source; it is fresh, alive, and spontaneous. It bubbles up from the fountain of life itself. It is full of wisdom, love, and truth. It radiates being. It is anchored in the present. Each breath is a source of wonder.

"Neti neti" (neither this nor that)

The inner seems to follow a different law. It unifies and even embraces opposites which boggle the logical mind based on dualistic principles of differentiation, either this or that, black and white. In the inner there is space for this and that, for both and. The needle is the symbol not the scissors.

"I am that"

One outcome of the connectedness with the true self is that it changes the outlook onto life. It becomes more life affirmative. One is falling in tune or even in love with the whole. The sense of being isolated and separate disappears and a sense of togetherness and of being one with the whole arises. One can feel the same life flowing in each and everything. There is acceptance of the other, be it people, animals, plants, rocks or stars. Everything is part of the whole. There is the sense of space for oneself and the other. The other is less of a potential danger one has to protect oneself from. The other rather turns into an opportunity to meet and unfolds into a source of enrichment, joy, love and creativity. Life resembles more an orchestra playing a symphony in harmony than a lonely tune in the jungle.

"I am life"

When the door opens to the inner it opens both ways, one dissolves and becomes more crystallized. Though there is nobody there one is crystallized as an individual whose uniqueness is deliciously tangible. Though we are all made of the same stuff, each one of us is totally unique and equipped with a unique brand of gifts. By looking in and letting go of what is not me I will discover these gifts by and by. It becomes easier to know what is what. One becomes more anchored in the present, grounded in the now. The need to change, defend or proof fades away. Lightness, playfulness, love and humor can spread. Life turns more in a mystery to be discovered than a problem to be solved. All quite wonderful! As the peaks are getting higher the valleys are becoming deeper.

"I am trust"

The borders between in and out become blurry, shift and dissolve. Resting in ones true abode even the body, emotions, feelings and thoughts can be experienced as the outer and only the witnessing awareness is in. The dewdrop is disappearing into the ocean.

Or one is so expanded that the whole world is sitting inside, one is all, the ocean disappearing into the dewdrop. Kabir (Indian Mystic) said: "My first experience was that the dewdrop is disappearing (into the ocean); my last experience is that the ocean has disappeared into me. Now I am the whole."

"I am nobody"

It takes some getting used to with this 'ongoing identity crisis' - as I like to call it sometimes (psychologist's and shrink's alarm bells flashing). There are no signboards inside not even a path. Nobody else can help not even ones own past experiences. The path is created as one goes.

"It's me"

How do I know what is true? No books, no studies are needed; just a bit of trust into ones own capacity of aware-ing, witnessing and sensing in the moment. It is not a question of knowledge but of being and being with what is. It is a trial and error situation. By being willing to make mistakes one takes the risk and stands behind the experience of the moment and learns through it. By and by the sense of what is true becomes more astute by seeing, feeling, tasting, touching and listening to who I am and what is in the moment. One gets rooted inside and trust grows. As the protective layers crumble one is vulnerable and strong at the same time. The clues for truth differ for each one of us. For some they are auditive, truth has a certain ring. For others they are kinesthetic, they feel it in their belly or heart; or they get goose bumps on the skin. The visuals see it clearly and follow the light. For others it's simply an inner knowing, a relaxation or a sense of ease inside. Of course these clues are not exclusive, any combination is possible. What they have in common is they are simple and rooted in the senses. Sensing is a direct experience in the present; it is happening now.

"I am bliss"

Looking in and sensing also means bringing the focus of awareness in. If I am lost on the outside oblivious of myself I will not be in touch with what is going on inside nor with who I am. The senses are a door in. And they are bridges between the outer and the inner, the mundane and the divine. From becoming aware of what I am aware of to being aware of who is it that is aware is not such a big step. But it is the step into the mysterious world of the true self.

Gate gate param gate parasam gate bodhi swaha
(gone, gone, completely gone, gone beyond)
Prajñaparamita mantra

Self

by Jayananda Maurizio Costantino

The light was that of Tuscany, an early afternoon at the end of May.

For weeks he had been feeling a tiredness he'd never felt before, a penetrating weakness, that stayed with him all day from first thing in the morning.

It was Sunday and five hundred kilometers awaited him for his journey back to

Trieste. Once decided, he heaved himself up from out of the armchair to go to the room where he had lived for the past few days. The window looked out onto the large courtyard of an old homestead on a hill and the light brought out the greens and blues of the old walls, the wooden floor, the objects which had now become familiar. He felt held back, in slow motion, in a world that was friendly and yet elusive, so little known.

He began to collect his things while he scoured the room to make sure nothing had been forgotten.

Then suddenly the center of his chest became hard without warning and there was an overpowering pain, cold, sweat and the suddenness of the unknown.

While putting on a sweater to try and shield himself he realised how little strength he had, only just enough.

He got up off the bed where he was sat and, in that faint wash of light, in great pain and disorientation, he said: "yes". And once he had said "yes", "yes, this is how it is", he stopped thinking and knowing, not asking and even less so explaining, from where this "yes" had come: Neither why, from where, nor how - full of pain inside - that "yes", really a "yes", emerged.

He stopped getting ready and turned towards the living room.

"I don't feel very well" he said, quietly to his close friend, without wanting to frighten him and with this he let himself drop onto the armchair.

The pain was overpowering. And he, he was in his breathing, as it went down into his stomach: light, fluid, calm and as big as the world.

I don't know. I don't understand what is happening to me.

I won't even ask what is happening to me.

Such little energy and breathing from the bottom of my belly causes me to let out a voice that is slow and careful while I ask for two drops of Bach Rescue. And I say to myself, and say to them, perhaps it would be better to call an ambulance.

Kapil looks at me, shocked, and Elena moves the cover aside in which I am wrapped and searches for my pulse. And, not just the cover is enfolding me, but everything: their caring anxiety, the air and the things in the living room, and the weakness that accompanies me as I lay down on the sofa.

I am the pain, the emptying out and this soft clarity. Everything is clear: I have no energy or time to judge, but just to exist. Everything is clear. Everything is.

They arrive. I hear the voice of the doctor, both warm and insistent: I ask her to speak more slowly and I sense all the concern flowing from her dark, extremely present eyes.

In the room, the nurses with their orange fluorescent jackets work painstakingly.

I am calm and not even surprised by my tranquility.... The room is like an aquarium and everyone moves, floating about in it, with total care regarding what is happening.

I trust.

I trust. I don't decide to trust. I just trust.

I put my trust in the world, relying on that subtle, delicate, dense being that I am at this moment.

I am an energy that is touched and smiling. I see that the others become aware of this and are somewhat surprised.

And I am touched, I smile and I am not at all surprised by my serenity.

And I trust the passion, compassion and knowledge of that doctor. But also I trust those twenty minutes in Accident and Emergency where two doctors, just a few meters away from my stretcher, speak together about football or that other doctor, in the second ambulance, who is much, much more afraid than me, while the siren attempts to get me through the traffic and the light is that of nightfall with the flashing reflections and I have time. I have time.

I am the time of being and I think of nothing.

I observe, see, observe, see, feel. At peace, and all the time feeling light throughout. With the pain.

It doesn't even seem strange to me, not even now, three years later that the word "heart attack" or "death" didn't flash into my mind.

The truth is that - at least at that moment - reality didn't need a name.

The truth was (is) everything I saw, felt, put in words, exchanged, existed.

The truth was (is) what existed, perhaps in a light stupor, and a witnessing without thought!

Only hours after, no longer in pain and safe, could I cry together with Kapil and Elena, as the past and future came into view once more.

And then the truth began to want words and names again.

Yes, the truth requires names. Names that imply, signify, express a question: "You too?"

You too? You too are here? Do you also suffer, feel happiness, fumble? Like me? With me? Truth is the need for endorsement by others: words, looks, gestures that take shape between the unceasing past and a sought after future... "You too?"

And therefore, I am also this: words, like those that I am writing, to be with you and reassure myself that I am with you.
Words of silence and/or the past/future; words that together with my odor, my movements, the thickness of my body, emerge, float, and gather together and embrace the world, and you.

Words that claim to be true because they are useful.

Words, or sounds, like *"The art of flight"* by Bach, played by Glenn

Gould at this moment, for me, or better, with me.

And since I am already well over the two thousand words you asked for in participating in your work, dear brother Avikal, I want to tell you another thing about me, about truth and about putting things into words.

It was 1995 and, for the first time I was in Pune, in India. I spent my days encountering many forms of meditation and taking in the sights of India, absorbed in the colors, the faces, the enjoyment of having time for myself. In the field of "meditation" I was, and I considered myself to be a total beginner.

One day, just before leaving, and after three weeks of sometimes funny, sometimes serious, discoveries, I took my courage in both hands and presented myself for meditation in what was Osho's old home. The thing that worried me most was knowing that it involved a one-hour meditation, in the dark, but above all kneeling. And I was really afraid of not being able to stay for one full hour on my knees, without moving !!!

But, as it was, I had encountered lots of encouragement up until this moment.....

I don't know how much time had passed. A question arose inside me. A question that, in twenty years of work with the mentally impaired - and with those who are in charge of their wellbeing - a question that I had asked myself many times. But in that moment it referred to a man, a patient, a prisoner who I had met in the mental hospital in Leros (Greece) where I had been working the previous year.

"Vassili. What bonded me so profoundly to him? It was not friendship, not at all like friendship as I know it. I haven't acted with him, for him, on him and his entire world, I certainly haven't acted in such an intense and personal way because of "work"!?

Not "friendship", not "work". Then what? It's a question that has been following me for twenty years - along with the faces of some, many people who have come into my life and left their mark.

And the response came. Unequivocal, so true that the question of "reflecting on it", evaluating it, thinking about it, imagining the consequences, was never raised and neither could I raise it.

And the reply, which in that instant seemed to arrive from who knows where, and which I assigned "naturally" to Osho was: love.

No pain in the knees. An hour of darkness had already passed.

Happiness, emotionally moved and smiling – that's right, so deeply touched and smiling! – in understanding with my heart and with my head, that that was the truth.

It was "love", yes, it was. This word took form; it evidenced itself inside me, acknowledging love. It was simple, like everything that's true.

A love that is about living in harmony together, in the same world.

It seems to me that it took some time, some weeks then, to become aware that the reply came right from myself, from my own Self. And only today perhaps, also the matter of its origin, and of other answers, no longer arises.

Two years later, in Poona, I was given the name (no/me!!??) with which I greet you and which signifies " benediction that descends from knowing oneself".

A discrete bow and smiling.

Relax, Don't Do It
by Shanasa van Raamsdonk

Since I can remember I have always been a "seeker".

Growing up in a socialist household, I was warned against Christianity, and any attempts to know more about religion were not encouraged. My parents saw religion as the evil of the world, and my dad hated the Pope, I was as I can remember very interested in something people described as God, or religion, and one of my early memories is me wanting to go to Bible classes. That was not allowed by my parents, they saw it as corruption of the mind.

By the time I was about 16, I was very impressed by Herman Hesse. Some of his books I read several times, my favorites were Narcissus and Goldmund and Siddhartha. He and Stevie Wonder became my first Gurus. Through them I got the first flavors of true self.

I did Yoga, Tai chi, massage workshops and Za Zen meditation, read Jung and Krishnamurti, became a vegetarian, and got interested in Reich an Alexander Lowen. Via Lowen's books, I got in touch with my first therapy groups, Bio Energetics and Encounter. I studied at a very experimental Drama school, got almost psychotic, and started to have chronic fear attacks.

My longing was very strong, but my mind was in fear.

In that time I got in touch with Osho, I did meditations in the Osho center and became friends with Sannyasins. I was amazed that a movement like that existed, it was everything I ever dreamt of. I was riding a high wave of love and expansion, and lived for a while in a radical Therapy and Transformation Commune. My highs and feeling of expansion grew bigger and bigger, I had hardly any sleep and felt ecstatic most of the time. I got initiated into Sannyas and got a new name. I felt I had come home...

After 18 months the highs turned into feelings of oppression, fearful and dark spaces, and I left, to move into a smaller commune, with kind of the same rules but more freedom.

After another year or so I was ready to meet the master in the flesh, and went to Pune. I got in touch with a much deeper space that I experienced before, I totally fell in love with Osho. I was only lucky enough to be with him for one year, and after he left his body, I spend the next 10 years most of my time in his commune.

I was still very thirsty and did group after group, and helped and assisted in many different group processes. That was my life, I loved it. I loved the deepness and the honesty of it, and felt I could be myself...In between I went to Holland to make money, and found it often hard to be "in the West" as we called it. It was hard to be the new me in a strange environment, I felt not "rooted" in the new me yet. I always felt there was something missing, that I was not complete, not in India, and not in the West.

By that time there was a small wave of people that declared themselves 'Awake' or 'Enlightened'. I remember being very fascinated by that, I was watching an interview of Satyam Nadeen talking about his experiences together with my friend, and we both were fascinated that 'one of us 'ordinary seekers' had become 'Enlightened'. I read his book later about his 'Awakening' with much enthusiasm. Via a close friend I came in contact with a Sannyasin who had declared herself 'enlightened'. She was inspired by Ganga-Ji and gave one to one spiritual guidance sessions to selected people.

She accepted to take me on, and we had a series of talks. She gave me tapes of Ganga-Ji to listen to, and on one tape somebody was describing his 'Awakening', and listening to that tape, I felt completely One with that experience.

I talked to my 'teacher' about that and she basically told me that I was now 'Enlightened'. I did not really know what to do with that, and was wondering how to behave now that I was 'Enlightened'. But of course my Ego really liked it, and claimed it immediately. I was too shy to give public satsangs, as my 'teacher' advised but otherwise I probably would have done that at that time. I spent a lot of time alone after that, sitting in my hanging chair, lying on my couch, reading Ramana, and only leaving my home to go shopping or to the swimming pool.

Looking back, I don't really know what happened there, it is probably true that I did have a 'recognition of true self'. I went to see Ramesh Balsakar (an Indian mystic in the Advaita tradition) in Bombay, and was just enjoying him talking and explaining his spiritual concept, basically the same 5 words over and over again: 'You are not the doer'. That simple concept hit me in the core of my being, and I really understood then and there that life just happens and little 'me' had absolutely no say in that. This pointer went really deep, it was not just an intellectual understanding, I felt like I was complete drenched in that understanding. Something really clicked and relaxed at that point.

I was wondering why people were there hanging around him for so long, because it seemed all so simple to me. I went to see Ramesh for about 3 days, and my friends who were with me said I should ask him some questions, but I just did not have any. I just enjoyed sitting there listening to him talking, and went aha, aha, yes, yes....It was the ultimate pointer to truth for me then, and still is now. It felt like all questions got dissolved in 'that" and I stopped asking. What stopped for me at that time is the running after truth or the desire for truth, I have no other way to describe it.

I used to believe that if I would work hard enough on myself and do group after group, I would eventually get somewhere.

I gave up looking for "it", and with that something relaxed inside, to a point that I was not interested at all anymore in techniques, satsangs and group processes. After many years being involved in group work that was probably what I needed. I enjoyed being "normal" and enjoyed doing ordinary things, and finally relaxed. Something deeply relaxed inside of me, and I felt so much spaciousness inside of me. I felt "unburdened" of the stress of seeking after truth. Until then there had always been a nagging feeling on the background, that there was something wrong with me, that I had to improve myself.

That feeling completely disappeared.

I have more patience and compassion for my flaws, and don't take them so personally anymore. I experience my true self and my false self every day, and I am watching the whole shebang unfolding. Sometimes I get very involved with my mind and my emotions, but mostly I can catch myself, lately more and more.

The last 9 years I have been living a simple life with not much desire for anything else. I have a strong sense of being carried by the whole, and living and working in the middle of the rain forest gives me a strong connection to the earth and myself. I feel content and at peace with what is.

In Service to the Movements of Being
by Attilio Piazza

While I am writing the snow is falling outside. It is the end of 2008, a year that I will remember as one of the most intense after the day of my birth in 1952 and that of my spiritual rebirth way back in 1979. Four adventurous cycles of seven years have passed since then, years in which gratitude, love and compassion were the sentiments that I surely lived the most, the longest and in good company. While writing to you I find myself in the midst of a wonderful new transition towards a new rebirth. Perhaps we could name this chapter the *Chronicles of Bardo*. For those who don't know the significance of Bardo, put simply, in Buddhist traditions Bardo is the period of transition from one incarnation to another. Let's immediately begin by mentioning that what dies is only the ego; the whole collection of ideas of ourselves and our lives that - if we think hard and often – we can make appear to be true. Who continues to live on, even during the transition, is that manifestation of a universal consciousness that is in continual evolution as life itself. And so what happens during Bardo? What happens is that some mental forms reveal their illusory nature, and then shatter, vanishing, leaving place for new emanations that in turn generate new life. Some aspects of the ego therefore dissolve enabling the being to become free. And this is how I feel I've spent a good part of the last 8 or 9 months, enjoying good health and enthusiasm.

And so, what is the story of the "true me" that I am getting ready to tell you about? It's the one in which I find myself surrendering myself to my smile: voice, face and movement of my soul. When I follow it I feel my being is moving in a direction of perfect harmony with Everything. Therefore, after much wandering and meandering in psychotherapy and thanks to years of meditation and lots of other things, for me things today are like this: if I smile to myself, than I

128

move in that direction. That's it. My winning decisions contain a smile, my choices are preceded by a smile that then sustains my action. I am learning to put my skills to the service of my smile. And when there is no smile, what happens? As far as I can see at the moment, its absence implies mistakes in evaluation either regarding direction or the way in which I turn my attention in the right direction: And in fact every time I take the trouble to look a bit deeper, or I note convictions that get in the way of progressing in a certain movement or I find that my being is already smiling at another that I hadn't noticed before. Evidently there is always something to smile about: You just have to know where to find it.

The other day one of my students was very happy with herself and she said to me: "Now I understand why change is called the way it is: Cambia Mento" (In Italian change is CAMBIAMENTO, Cambia comes from the verb 'cambiare' which means to change. And Mento literally means chin.) "Change your Chin, and that is to say: if I follow my chin, I will change direction!" Clever! I thought, providing the chin follows the movement of the heart! And that's it, and at this point as far as I'm concerned there's nothing else to add, apart from we can't live on smiles alone… In my opinion we suffer when we are not aware of the changes in motion. This is a mistake that I have made many times: I think of myself as being in a certain way while, in reality, inside me I fail to see that movement is in progress.

For years I have worked at giving more space to one of my qualities, that of teaching others what I have learned: It is a way of sharing my being with that of another person and, together, to be truer and freer. About a year ago, I felt the impulse to expand this communion that happens through teaching to a larger number of people. Assuming that this impulse wasn't a desire; that is to say it didn't manifest a possible aspect of the ego such as thirst for fame or desire for more money or other such things, assuming also then that there was an authentic movement in action: I needed to understand that I couldn't let this change happen while remaining exactly as I was. Something also had to change in me. In hindsight, and I had taken a little to realize it, what had to change was a limited idea of who "I" was, and I had no idea of the inner journey that awaited me. For years I had thought of myself as teacher: I Am A Teacher. Looking at my future I thought that I would continue to become a better teacher etc. This idea distracted me when I felt I the need to develop an organizational structure capable of sustaining this impulse for the expansion of my teaching. Thus the first evaluative mistake: I need a new organizational structure, but I can stay as I am. The "pains" began when I began to hear (from others!) that in order to sustain the development in the way necessary, not only was an organizational structure required but also a strong and dynamic administrative and financial business structure. Nooooo ! All these things nooo! I don't want administration. I really don't! I am a teacher. I am. And here is the problem: "I am a teacher, I". And so, month after month, consultation after consultation, meditation after meditation, I surrendered to the fact that, not only did I find myself already in a new transition, but that I had to think of myself in a different way from how I had thought of myself in the last three cycles of seven years: Not only a teacher, but manager of a company of teachers. Here I am, with another sigh ready to greet the new world. New world? But if the company had always been there, and if there are loads of people that do that work there, where is the newness? The newness is that I don't have the minimum idea of how this thing works. And, among other things, those few ideas available "on the market" didn't seem so great. And so? And so either I meditate, or meditate, or alternatively I meditate. And why not? Because, for me, it is from a state of meditative consciousness that new things can be born; something new that is in tune with the spirit of freedom, the longing for peace to which we all aspire, students and teachers alike, and that – will permit – allow my soul to smile. And so let's immediately carry out an experiment and verify how this story of the smile works when actually applied to the development of a project:

1) If I don't allow the expansion of my teaching to a large number of sentient beings, do I smile? No. If I think about all the extra people who will benefit from the expansion of my work, do I smile? Yes. Therefore the expansion has to be "done".

2) If I facilitate the expansion and only keep teaching? No, I don't smile. If I go ahead with the expansion, take a deep breath and look after the organizational teaching structure, do I smile? Yes. Good, so then I'll make a start. And so the organizational structure goes ahead.

3) Can I develop the necessary teaching structure here in Italy, without creating a company with an administration and financial structure to support it? No. It would be too stressful. And if I take the responsibility for setting up business, administrative and financial support: To at least understand how it works, to find out who to collaborate with; how to create an organizational support structure that will best develop my teaching? With another deep breath, the answer is: "yes, of course", and I feel much better. I feel it, and smile.

That's it. As far as I'm concerned I have no choice. This is my destiny that is creating itself, and the only suffering comes from the idea that it shouldn't be like this. I just recognize these ideas and then let it dissolve into nothingness, while the new takes shape. This is the Bardo I told you about in which I find myself.

There is something that connects who writes this book with who reads it: we are all interested in how to live in the truth, freedom and love that we already are.

I hope I have inspired trust and respect for the unknown that manifests itself through us, creating our life in infinite forms. Suffering? It is in opposing the movement of the soul and of inadvertently using obsolete mental-forms in the emerging reality.

It was wonderful to think of Avikal and of you readers while I was writing this. Good luck in your quests.

Out of the Carousel
by Rani Willems

I remember one of my first experiences of being very well. I was participating in an awareness intensive retreat and spent the first 24 hours turning round and round in my mind, trying to answer the question: Who am I? In the process my mind became exhausted and all of a sudden out of nowhere I was somehow outside of the mind. I saw that turning mind as a very colorful carousel, a great carnival, a never ending movement of thought and emotion, sometimes fun, sometimes sad, sometimes angry or fearful. I got fascinated with the watching of it. I remember cracking up again and again about the colorfulness of it all. What a show!! And then probably some hours later, another shift happened. I no longer was interested in what I witnessed but in the witnessing itself. It was as if my whole existence imploded into one huge pool of a unified experience which I later named Being. Just to be here filled my body with a deep silence. My mind became crystal clear, it was as if I could see through the past and future, I became more aware of my body and it was as if it filled with substance. I remember that all of a sudden it felt like I had more weight, I was more grounded and certainly more Here and Now.

In fact it felt like here and now was the only option there had ever been, only I had missed it!!! Great laughter arose when I realized that all my seeking and searching had been in the wrong direction. What a cosmic joke. All I had ever wanted was here; right here and right now and my body seemed to be the vehicle for it all. As the awareness intensive retreat took several days there were openings upon openings. At some point I became acutely aware of the spontaneous movement of the universe. It was having its own rhythm, like the waves in the ocean. No one was making the waves yet they were moving. No one was pushing or doing and it all happened in utmost harmony. It was a big opening and at the time it overwhelmed me cause it was so new and I was not used to being so big. I saw perfection everywhere, even in war and sickness. I was baffled.

Over the years the experience of being deepened and became more present in my day-to-day activities. It lost its overwhelming-ness and started to feel more and more natural. A lot of integration was needed so that the gap between being "in the mind" or being in my personality and being was not so big anymore Slowly my personality got infused with the different qualities of being and in that it became more transparent and porous. Now when I stay connected to being, life is easy, everything flows, whatever happens, happens. I meet life as it comes without resistance. When there is no sense of separation there is nothing to resist!!! There is connectedness. So there is a natural responding to whatever life brings. When I disconnect because of one trigger or another, I bump into things and people, I sense walls, there is separation again. My mind, who just before, in the experience of being, was a good servant to me, a great help in managing my daily life, bringing the practicalities together for me, takes back its central place as the boss, the one who runs my life. All of a sudden I am not guided anymore by a vertical alignment but I am guided by thoughts, and their driven-ness. And then, tension reminds me that I have left being. When that happens, it is usually followed by a natural movement of sinking back into the body, and a discharge of the superfluous energy of stress, followed by deep sighs or even yawning and I am resting back in myself and can continue my daily activities in a connected way. This is the dance of my life. As I learn to not resist the shifting back and forth in and out of being, the riddle dissolves.

A Light onto Myself
by Kapil Nino Pileri

While settling down to write I observed the emerging of an inner dialogue relative to witnessing my experience during these years of intense practice of presence. Witnessing is bringing attention to myself and observing my mind that is continually looking for objects, ideas, opinions and not myself. Witnessing is putting myself at the center of my attention and becoming conscious of my existence, of how I function, what my motivations are, and how doing it causes me to recognize myself in the present moment, right now. And, also, recognizing that memories and past events, emerging from the past, give me a point of view in which everything is filtered by the knowledge I have through what I have already experienced : filters of pain and fear that, like slides, continue to project themselves onto the screen of my present, overshadowing and making it into something I must defend myself from and making me believe that I'm something mechanical, fixed, that reacts to reality and is afraid of life, rather than living. Witnessing is not worrying about the future and not thinking: What shall I do next? Where am I going? What shall we do with this? But, on the contrary, it is using the situation so as to integrate it within me rejoicing in the splendor of mystery.

I turn my attention to my felt sense of being and I realize that my search is no more, and all my attention and consciousness are concentrated on letting everything arrive before me without effort and letting everything that arrives go, one moment after the other; beyond perception itself there is my true energy, which I live one drop at a time, incorporating the fact that sometimes I still need to be there and listen to it and live it, to understand, observing it. Being with the paradox of saying I AM and knowing that I can't point this out or explain it verbally leaves me free to abandon my tendency to try and define myself. No images or definitions that refer to the physical manifestation of my body and to its expressions, words, emotions, I stand in the present in order to see and understand my conditioning. This is the natural state of being myself without identifying with anything, it is the natural unfolding of my true energy and natural state, without effort. When I am in my truth, I am: there is just being open to what emerges, the freedom of being and there is flow, there is lightness.

I remember the first Satori retreat that I took part in and how I arrived without even knowing what it was, trusting a friend who took care of me during that very intense time in my life, on the one hand weighed down by failure that was affecting every aspect of my life, economically, emotionally and relationship-wise and, on the other hand, that was opening up an overflowing abundance of new relationships and the opportunity to create a new life for myself in the way that I wanted, to suit myself, based on my wishes and creative passions. I went to the retreat specifically, because the advice received involved specifically working with Avikal, one of the teachers. Immediately I projected my father on him and all the rage that I had because he was dead and because he had left me: a projection that lasted for a good few years. I had already done this with other men older than me who I had met in the course of daily life and whose friendship, help or advice I continued to refuse, clouded as I was by the memories of past betrayal. At the same time I felt a type of melancholy and trust, something puzzling that became, later on, an important experience for me: consciousness of an inner space that opens up, and the capacity to maintain it intentionally, together with friendliness towards myself. Here I rediscovered my heart and realised that the damned self-judgment that I had about myself me – that I didn't have a heart – had finally dissolved in the recognition of how much love I felt. To be friendly towards myself is fundamental in the course of the sessions I give and it is a discovery that continues to go deeper, as I continue to practice presence and self-inquiry. I realised that in all those years, Avikal had done none other than be there for me, instinctively open, and I realised that my reaction expressed itself with an inner sense of hostility and various attempts of flight. And here arrives an immense sense of gratitude for him and, through this, for life itself and for the practice of awareness. God how much passion for this work! Still, when I think of the universe he comes to mind. Clearly in all this I also observed that when I am in contact with my heart, without expectations or mental planning (alas, another weak point for me: my mind would like to pre-programme everything), the path becomes clear and evident. A path that is full of commitments and hard work but also of results and satisfaction. Through my work I can see where I am truly passionate and complete, whether with groups or in individual sessions: I work and expand myself in understanding and presence with a boundless energy that expresses itself through creativity and openness.

In that first Satori I also met Ganga, a woman who I consider to be my other teacher: I can't forget the sensation, of "sitting" for the first time in my life, facing her: the experience of the force of gravity, of being simply here without reason, on this earth, and not floating in mid air, carried by the moods of the past winds or of how others wanted me to be, and the sensation of being able to stop making dramas and complaining to myself. I saw my image and I realised that I am the one who sees, I am consciousness, without conditioning or drama, without an attachment to unhappiness and having to be angry to be able to feel myself: yes, I am consciousness and dis-identification. And I discovered through working with her, work that still continues, a kindness towards myself, that is slowly, slowly expanding also out towards others. Loving kindness, down-to-earth compassion and the opportunity to forgive myself and accept myself for what I am and to join in the meetings with others without judgments or preconceptions, with an open heart. It is incredible how this experience of the heart has been, and continues to be, so intense and in continual expansion. Lately I experience it in a new and light way, as a particular quality of the moment and of being present: I feel like I'm a candle that ignites itself by going close to the fire and now shines brightly itself. Yes, I feel that after having learnt to stand on my own feet, the intensity makes me be a light onto myself, a radiance of my own energy, passion and presence.

I recognize and observe the will to continually practice presence, even at the cost of making mistakes, falling down and getting back up again, of experimenting with myself, of keeping my inner space open and available, without judgment. Alert, I continue to search, to inquire, interrogating myself continually, dedicating myself to myself, listening to my fear and recognizing it as a self-defense mechanism and letting myself go through it, hanging on to nothing, staying face to face with myself without separation, without thinking about what I could do the next time.

In recent years I have also undergone training on the Inner Judge and I have felt, seen and tasted the disappearing, and finally absence, of that unexplainable tension that had worn me out and accompanied me for such a big part of my life, causing me to worry so much, trying to programme and control, not allowing me to feel free and isolating me inside the hard and impenetrable shell of a nut, tethering myself to those images of me, stale and discolored.

I enjoy meeting others, learning, I am inquisitive. Meeting others gives me the opportunity to carry on being, to stay in the present. Presence and compassion are what I naturally feel emerging in the sessions and with the groups, lightly, from my Being. Many times my clients have said that the simple feeling of being in the sessions with me, in a space without judgment, reconnects them with their own flow of vital energy: this is the miracle.

Consciousness and vitality express themselves and flow together and interconnected, integrated in my everyday life. I feel like I've climbed many inner mountains, and my legs are ready to climb even higher ones.

My Experience of Getting to My True Self
by Mark Gleeson

My experience getting to my true self is reflected in my search for truth and my truth. Just after sleep some mornings as I am now, I feel closer to being in what I regard as my truth. I began my personal search for the truth in my infancy after an occurrence that is described later in this chapter. Being asked to write about what truth is has intensified my search and my articulation of what truth is to me. So what is the truth? Words can be important here. Are we talking about *the truth* or in other words, the absolute truth or am I talking about *my experience of the (absolute) truth* or are we talking about *my experience of what truth is for me*. I am writing here about *my experience of what truth is for me*. The first aspect of truth for me is deeply embedded in how I get to truth. The how I get to truth is always the door to the truth for me. The feeling of absolute clarity about some aspect of my being/truth/reality and even what I presume to be the true nature of a human being has always come to me during or after movement. Movement is how I get to my experience of truth. My being reaches aspects of my truth during or after running, swimming, walking, dance, ecstatic dance, active meditation, Feldenkrais, during breath-work and in one situation while rocking like a baby in a deep state of regression. Moving does something very profound for me and assists me to reach states of clarity about what truth is for me. These states of clarity are seemingly camouflaged from me when I am not moving. The movement allows the camouflage netting to be lifted away and there I am in an undeniable state of personal truth and reality. A reality that can be stark, clear, obvious and always with a strong deep feeling and a sense that I am at home inside. A home which is my truth.

My history in one paragraph is that I have lived for most of my life in self sabotage with a companion called the inner critic (superego). The part of the personality or self known as the inner critics specializes in criticizing true feelings and also criticizes me for having the substitute feelings that are not real and not my truth. The resulting double bind limits my ability to act, move in a particular direction and be more of who I am. This inner critic has determined my mood states, my sense of self, my experience of my identity and has disempowered my ability to live in my truth. So far, the inner critic has kept me smaller than what I feel I am. This separation from my truth and reality has kept my heart in fear and away from commitment to almost everything, including a personal relationship based on truth. The commitment I do have, and have always had, is to follow a very strong desire to go beyond this perceived lack of reality and lack of truth. This is stronger than the program to not commit, as I am deeply committed to be, live, love and work in a meaningful and truthful way. So I am committed to formal practice of meditation most days, watching my self and my awareness of self as much as I can, moving and exercising most days and doing ongoing personal growth. I don't regard doing these activities or retreats like satori, where I expose areas of my personality that are not in truth, as work. These experiences can be as difficult as waiting for and having serious work done at the Dentist. After the dental work is finished and after these meditations I feel better and closer to my experience of what truth is for me.Why do I seek my truth and my true self? I have a clear gut feeling that my psychological experience during most of my life is not completely the real me. Only part of how I am being in the world at the moment is my self living in truth. What was presented to me in the womb, in early childhood and then reinforced in school, family and culture have not delivered me to a place I call the truth. My responses and reactions to what was presented to me initially didn't take me closer to an experience of my true self. These responses and reactions, in retrospect, took me closer to an avoidance of myself at unconscious levels. I constructed some very intelligent masks and veils to protect my ego. These masks and veils have been and are being exposed, piece by piece, in an ongoing process. A nice 'reframe' for this was provided by Osho when he said 'Non-truth was just a preparation so that truth can enter'(1978, p.265). I would add that for truth to enter, motivation is required for me to allow it to enter at conscious and unconscious levels. 'My hand is forced', in terms of motivation, to some degree, because the separation I feel from my true self is always being criticized by my inner critic. In my current personality structure, I have an inner critic that is banging on my head when I continue living with old dysfunctional patterns of behavior. In other words, my separation from the truth is being acknowledged and criticized by my inner critic. Maybe that is why I have incredible motivation to move away from programmed stuckness and stay on this spiritual path. I am not always clear, however, how to completely let go of 'non-truth' beyond continuing to be in the world with awareness.The hardest and the best part of increasing levels of awareness, is that I am more acutely aware of when I am not being in my true self. It is an interesting point whether I have to compromise my true self on some occasions to be in the world, particularly the corporate world, or whether the world is the truth and part of me isn't accepting some aspects of truth. For me getting to the truth has some environmental considerations. To get some clarity to commence writing, I have chosen to begin this writing in quite a beautifully furnished hotel suite. It is a clear space – a tastefully furnished suite of cream and white with natural morning light streaming in through the windows. My living space at home isn't always clear. There are small jobs and chores that could be done in many parts of the house. The outer clutter can mirror the inner clutter of my mind. If the outer or inner clutter is at too high a level, the truth is cluttered by layers of psychological and physical clutter. I suppose this is the 'dust on the mirror' that I have heard Osho speak about.

I am not the mask, the dust, the clutter and, therefore, these are not part of my truth. At this stage I am wondering what am I doing having masks, dusts and clutter in my life. My journey is clearly to get rid of them which is why I have done so many therapist trainings, satori retreats and personal growth groups. In one sense, these trainings and groups are 'rubbish removal' programs and in another sense, for moments and sometimes minutes, I have had the fortune to glimpse my truth in a clear mirror during or just after an active meditation, an exercise in Satori, a feldenkrais lesson. Sometimes my experience of the truth arises at a moment in everyday life outside of these activities. The biggest immediate awakening for me is always that the truth, as reflected in my true self, has been there all along. Underneath the dust, the clutter, the critic and the confused programs, the true self patiently waits. My experience of my truth is that it has certain characteristics. The first characteristic is an absolute certainty in my whole being and in what I experience as my self that some thought and feeling in my bodymind is actually the case. No further exploration is required and I am at the baseline of a particular experience.

The second characteristic is one of two feelings that occurs milliseconds or almost simultaneously with the first feeling. The first of these feelings is one of elation and a high in my whole body that I have uncovered something that has been with me for a long time. The morning after a Satori retreat, I was swimming laps in the Mullumbimby pool and I had a sentence come to me that enlightenment is when I am free of my conditioning. Without getting into what enlightenment is or is not, just imagining being in the world and free of conditioned patterns of behavior gives me a great sense of freedom and possibility of experiencing my true self. The second feeling is one of profound sadness. Sadness that a set of circumstances has produced a mindset and beliefs which are completely false. Sadness that I have been deceiving myself completely in ignorance for a long time. Sadness that I have living and being in a particular way that I honestly believed was *the truth* and *my true self* and it is not either. The sadness from this can last for days as the psyche (bodymindspirit) adjusts to the reality of self deception and the emptiness or 'hole' that remains. I had one such occasion when I experienced what I understand to be the 'great betrayal' during the *Born Again* process. Lying on the ground with a rug and sucking my thumb I regressed very clearly to a time in the backyard of our house when I was younger than walking age. I wanted to crawl and do something my own way and what I was told, or what I felt, was that that wasn't the way. There was the parental 'right' way. I resisted and was told again and I resisted and was told again. The pain was that my way or *my* true self could not be lived. The message was that it had to be someone else's truth to survive. My way wasn't the 'right' way, could never be the 'right' way and will never be the 'right' way. My feeling at that point was that I will have to betray myself to survive. I was sad and even sadder about my sadness for days. The realization was made that my truth and my true self that I felt in every cell in my body was not the 'right' way if I was to survive.

Two things are apparent about what I decided as a preverbal infant following this 'betrayal'. I decided I will have to live in separation from my truth to survive and I will resist and rebel against this separation. Writing this chapter, has made it clear, I haven't stopped resisting and rebelling against separation of my truth and I can survive in my truth. The 'betrayal' has been great and not complete.

Reference: Rajneesh, B.S. *The Discipline of Transcendence: Discourses on the 42 sutras of Buddha. Volume 1.* Rajneesh Foundation,1978 p. 265

Through the mirror
by Kya Ida Panicelli

When I believed that I'd put in order a large part of the conflicts that I had come across in the course of my life (father, mother, sister, and the irrepressible personality with which I have been endowed, they were the obstacles most grueling), a new conflict arose three years ago, unexpected and brutal, with the person that I had, up until then, considered to be my most intimate, trusted and treasured friend. A conflict that had to do with a broken agreement of trust and mutual recognition, and that revealed itself to be destructive beyond all measure.

The surge of initial anger for what I experienced as a betrayal on her part was overwhelming; I was absolutely incensed and bedeviled by the rage and internal commotion that broke out within me. The memories of the past years emerging in relentless waves, all confirming my own view of past events and that my decision to end the relationship was the right one. And the way in which my internal dialogue developed was one of the most commonplace, predictable and pointless: "she said, I said". Worse than a vicious circle, it is a tunnel without end. From there, there is no way out, it's like having a nest of serpents in your head....we get tangled up in the convolutions of the mind, and this only leads to further suffering.

There was no way of getting away from this tidal wave. The only thing I could do was consciously observe what emotions arose and what the sensations in my body were, and, despite being in the middle of the turmoil, to continue to trust the voice that was saying: 'go inside', the voice of the Self that was guiding me.

Inside my body this turmoil manifested itself as a tight knot in my stomach, an aching in my heart and a restlessness of my limbs, as well as a general sensation of uneasiness, due to an excessive heat that I felt all over my body: the heat was outside and inside, an incredible quantity of energy moving about inside, and burning, burning, burning with rage...

I went on like this, beating myself with the pain of loss and the obstinacy of my wounded pride, grappling with resentment, frustration, and a solid wall of reproach. Until my body led me to a place that was to prove decisive: the thermal spas of Ischia. It was summer, it was scorching, the water was extremely hot and bubbling, and I could only manage to stay in the bath for an hour in that heat; the same heat that I felt inside. The osmosis between the internal and external heat was one of the most intense sensations I have ever felt. I was one with the heat. It seemed to me that it was me who was heating the water....!

In that situation, where my body could finally relax into a 'like' medium, like in homeopathic treatment, a sort of transformation began to take place. I came into contact with what I call my red Kali, a quality that I feel very alive in me, that on a superficial level, concerns my anger and revenge, but on a more profound level, justice. Accepting that part of me; a part that has always frightened me because of its extreme connotations and potential for destruction, was very difficult. At times the goddess Kali is depicted, in a very real way, as a female figure running; red tongue protruding from her mouth, cutting down heads and bodies with her sword, in a devastating fury from which there is no escape. She terrorized me and at the same time I couldn't avoid her energy that felt obscure but vibrant. I tried to get away, but I continued to feel her hot breath on me. I felt I was confronting the darkest part of me, and even though attempting to keep my inner image of the calm and aloof meditator intact, there was no way of eluding myself. It was clear at that point the conflict with my friend had receded to the background. The conflict was now between me and me...And until I kept fighting there was only suffering. But after much resistance,

I surrendered, I resigned myself to the darkness, I said yes to it. It happened between one moment and the next, with an unexpected relaxation that spread throughout my body, together with the awareness that I could look with my eyes open into the darkness, that also that darkness was 'me', that until I accepted it and included this part of me, all my meditating would be just a fruitless endeavor.

The sensation was that of opening my arms in front of a black mirror and saying: come on, show yourself, reveal yourself fully. Then the inner image shattered, but also the fear dematerialized and, from inside, out came new courage. Surprised, looking inside at that darkness that I had feared so much, I discovered that the conflict had gone, and an opening in space, a being attentive, a sharper observance of internal movements and their significances, and again an acceptance without reserve of everything that was, moment after moment. The energy seemed transformed: I was able to own the conflict with my friend, the dark part of me, while my relaxation became deeper and deeper, my acceptance ever greater.

But there was another transition yet to go through. Recognizing the magnitude of loss for myself wasn't sufficient: if I hadn't found the courage to share it with her, this recognition would have remained an unfinished event, a half realization. And then I took the step that was missing: I telephoned her. Down went another part of my self-image! I knew that I was abandoning every certainty of being able to control events. I was entering into new, unknown and uncertain territory, without knowing what I might find at the other end of the telephone, with no guarantee of goodwill on the part of my friend, without knowing whether I would be attacked again, without knowing, without knowing... And in this new territory without a map I wasn't experiencing distance and separation anymore, but on the contrary, connection and trust. The story about Milarepa came to mind who, in a demonstration of trust in his Master, threw himself over a cliff, and I felt just like this, also I was falling from the cliff and the strange thing was that it struck me that I wasn't afraid anymore, and there was no conflict. I had simply arrived there. What a relief.

Staying connected with my body was essential, everything anchored to presence, the moment. Today I still remember the physical sensations that I experienced as I dialed her telephone number, hearing the sounds of water as I walked by the side of the torrent, the smell of rain after a storm, I see the branches of the oaks, under my fingertips I can feel the sensation of the silky chestnut shell that was in my hand at the time, like a firm rock to which I was anchored, with all my senses alight and alert...

And the words came from an empty space that I felt in my belly, not empty as in absence, but empty like silence, as the words came out on their own out of the silence. The connection between feeling and communicating was there, clear as crystal, in direct alignment between belly, heart and mind. Finding words that were faithful to my feelings in the here and now, declaring where I was and what my intentions were, asking forgiveness for my errors and offering peace, without expecting results, but remaining open to all possibilities, it was an experience carried out by presence, precise, authentic, crystalline.

It wasn't the end of our disagreement: our friendship wasn't revived from the ashes out of the blue; there were other steps to take to get nearer. We are still in the process, so to speak. But now, finally, it has created space between us, we can once again communicate from the heart.

Successively, in fact, in continuing to observe, I have been able to also 'see' things from my friend's point of view, and then to see that my pain was like hers, and that what I had lost; losing our friendship, our partnership and trust, she had lost too. Little by little, my compassion for her and for me, for our pain, has come afloat. What was turmoil in my belly has settled into a lake in my heart, where sadness and nostalgia have manifested, then acceptance and compassion, and finally also gratitude for everything that's good and beautiful, everything we have come across in the twenty years of our friendship. And I wanted once again to share with her this last transition, honoring the beauty and the profoundness of what we have shared over the years, honoring our story and the truth of feeling. Feeling her pain inside me has melted away residual black lumps for ever. Empathy revealed itself as the key for overcoming our disagreement.

Consciousness has accompanied me throughout my entire journey, whether in rage and pain, or in relaxation. I have learnt to listen to and trust the voice of my inner guide, but even more I have learned to trust my body, which like an infallible map guides me to the truth of the moment.

Appendix

CATHARSIS, MEDITATION
AND EVOLUTIONARY THRUST

*Merriam-Webster's definition of Catharsis (from the Greek word
Katharsis) "a purification or purgation that brings about spiritual
renewal or release from tension"*

When we are on the path that leads to the discovery of our True
Nature, through our meditations, through inquiry and the physical
exercises that we do, through visualizations, we dive into our
unconscious and reactivate the material that was originally
repressed.

In childhood, the way in which we separated and disconnected
from parts of ourselves considered dangerous and unacceptable
was initially a process of suppression. Suppression means that
things to be avoided are cancelled and rejected, but still accessible
to our conscience. This process generates pain in the child and a
concomitant desire/need to avoid pain which causes something
more radical to begin: repression. Repression means that those same
unacceptable materials are not only negated and refused but are
buried in the unconscious and forgotten about and hence they are
no longer accessible to the conscious mind. In short, we lay a rock
on top of them and completely forget. This enables us to not feel the
pain of the separation from essential qualities of our Being anymore
and, in the end, from our True Nature in its entirety.

A fundamental and inevitable part of remembering oneself
and of recovering these qualities and potentialities abandoned in
childhood involves the process of cathartic purification. Through
the light of our consciousness we revisit our history (and story),
we observe our present and our experiences, we explore the beliefs

and prejudices that that we keep carrying on, we shed light on the automatism of self-judgment, we do a huge amount of cleaning and detoxification.

We detoxify our bodies, our emotions, our minds, freeing our souls from unconscious identifications. All the material that we haven't digested, that doesn't belong to us, that has poisoned our system comes afloat and this is CATHARSIS. And this is exactly what we want because as this material floats up it is exposed to our consciousness and we have the opportunity to let go of those things that don't belong to us, that are false, harmful, old and poisonous. The final result is the manifestation of a new way of perceiving ourselves and the reality around us, a way that is purified and liberated from the past and is receptive to the intrinsic unity of existence: A way that doesn't need to divide and compare and negate parts of our internal or external reality because they are considered inappropriate and unacceptable.

It is a widespread preconception that maintains that meditation is a state of absolute peace and relaxation and that if it isn't like this then it isn't meditation. If you have ever tried to meditate, for example doing Vipassana or Zazen, or even quite simply sitting in silence with your eyes closed, then you will most certainly have experienced a great flood of thoughts, emotions and physical sensations, just when you were thinking and hoping to spend a little time in peace with yourself.

Osho gives a very delightful example of this when he talks about trying to stop the mind. Try, he says, and decide you're not going to think about monkeys for the next five minutes and you'll see, suddenly all the monkeys on the planet are interested in you, trampling over each other in an effort to get into your mind, until the five minutes have passed and you can finally say: now that's enough, and switch your attention to something else. And the monkeys disappear.

Meditation isn't stopping the mind, but rather about observing without participating in any way in the catharsis that happens moment by moment, like sitting on a beach watching the waves. At the beginning of our inner journey the waves will be very large and contaminated: don't run off, don't say: "it can't work because I'm not quiet or calm", stay present and observe WITHOUT GRASPING OR REJECTING, don't waste time commenting, simply let everything be exactly as it is. Catharsis is necessary and only after a little cleansing and detoxification will you begin to feel the gaps and the silences and your body relaxing. We have accumulated a large quantity of ideas, concepts, emotions, prejudices, that aren't part of us and to which we are very attached. To understand that catharsis is exactly the DEMONSTRATION THAT CHANGE IS HAPPENING, it's absolutely necessary if we really want to find our True Nature. And this realization helps us enormously in defending ourselves consciously from the attacks of the superego. Therefore one objective of our meditations, visualizations and inquiry is to reinforce our ability to be present with and through the chaos and upheaval that occur as a result of our search for truth.

The development of our ability to be with what there is, without interfering, keeping alive our passion and commitment to remember and find ourselves, is the ground on which, from a certain point onwards, we will be able to recognize the intrinsic evolutionary force of reality and the way in which we participate in this evolution. When we no longer make divisions between what is acceptable and appropriate and what is not, whether in ourselves or the world around us, then we are able to recognize and observe the movement of life without resistance and suddenly, this clear vision acknowledges that "everything simply happens" and that we are an intrinsic part of that "happening". From victims of time and life we can become participating and enthusiastic actors, and, perhaps, we can feel the happiness of our soul as it recognizes its cosmic place and the goal of its existence within this form.

"Being is dynamic. This dynamism manifests the richness of Being, inherent in us as the potentialities of ourselves, and because this nature is our nature, it moves our experience towards greater optimization. In

other words, the dynamism of Being impels and guides the self towards greater revelation of its potentialities, towards manifesting its primordial wholeness. So it is an evolutionary force that moves the self towards greater clarity, luminosity, creativity, depth, expansion, individuation, richness, and so on".[22]

"Rabbi Hanoch told this story:

"There was once a man who was very stupid. When he got up in the morning it was so hard for him to find his clothes that at night he almost hesitated to go to bed for thinking of the trouble he would have on waking. One evening he finally made a great effort, took paper and pencil and as he undressed he noted down exactly where he put everything he had on. The next morning, very well pleased with himself, he took the slip of paper in his hand and read: "cap" – there it was, he set it on his head: "pants" – there they lay, he got into them: and so it went until he was fully dressed. "That's all very well, but now where am I myself?" he asked with great consternation. "Where in the world am I?" He looked and looked, but it was a vain search; he could not find himself. "and that is how it is with us," said the rabbi".[23]

[22] Almaas A.H., The Point of Existence, p. 48
[23] *Buber Martin, The Way of Man – Ten Rungs, pages 26, 27*

Biography of Contributing Authors

Rafia Morgan

Conditioned in the USA, educated at UC Berkeley, has been involved in spiritual and cultural transformation since the 60's. He lives his life in wonder of the unfoldment of Being, in himself, in others and in the world around him. He has been blessed to be a disciple of Osho for the last 30 years. He is the founder of the work known as The Path of Love.

(www.pathoflove.net)

Anna Zanardi

I work as a journalist, writer, psychologist, therapist and organiza-tional consultant. My exploration during the last 45 years has led me to do many different things, with great passion and emotional intensity. I try to make myself useful, and if I am liked too that's a luxury. I love to laugh and I love travelling, being with my husband and son and having all my friends around me.

(www.annazanardi.com)

Ganga Cording

Holds an MA in Psychology, worked as a Clinical Psychologist and as a body-worker in Hara Awareness Massage, Psychic Massage and Rebalancing. She leads Awareness Intensive Retreats worldwide since over 30 years and is the founder of the Academy of Awareness and Creative Expression. She lives in Corfu.

(www.awareness-academy.com)

Jayananda Maurizio Costantino

He is incurably Sicilian. He holds a degree in Social Psychology from the School Of Advanced Studies and Social Sciences in Paris. He has been a teacher, publicist, psychologist, and primarily, a social

worker for a variety of public mental hospitals and other institutes of social confinement (beginning in 1976 in Trieste with Franco Basaglia, and also working for many years in France, Greece and Mozambique). Currently he is engaged with being at peace with himself in this world.
(www.outofsilence.worldpress.com)

Shanasa van Raamsdonk
Shanasa is 52 years old, happily married and living with his beloved Nishanto and Yoshi the dog in a community of friends in the middle of the beautiful rain forest of Mullumbimby, Australia. He and Nishanto are producing and selling silk clothing on markets and festivals.
(www.silkzdesign.com.au)

Attilio Piazza
Using his gifts of clarity and sensitivity acquired over twenty years of conducting seminars and formation courses, he teaches the technique of awareness, integrating meditation with the creative and productive capacities of contemporary man. He runs personal and professional formation courses in the Centro Studi Piazza based in Milan with the aim of furthering and promoting innovative educative processes for the development of human potential.
(www.centrostudipiazza.org)

Rani Willems
Rani has been on the path of inner transformation since 1976. For more than 30 years she has been sharing her experience in workshops and retreats.
(www.rani-willems.org)

Kapil Nino Pileri
He has practiced and taught Craniosacral therapy for many years, and facilitates Awareness Intensive Retreats: "Who am I?", and

Satori, as well as seminars on the Inner Judge. As part of this work he also offers individual sessions in various Italian cities, spending much of his time working and travelling, predominantly with people who are stepping into the world of spirituality and self-research for the first time.
(www.craniosacral-training.it)

Vartan Mark Gleeson
Vartan currently lives in Canberra, Australia watching the challenge of allowing his true self to unfold while working in organizational consulting, facilitating and a small psychology practice.

Ida Kiya Panicelli
She holds a degree in History of Arts completed at Rome University. After having worked as curator at the National Gallery of Modern Art in Rome, during the eighties, she edited ARTFORUM, an international contemporary art magazine, in New York from 1987 to 1992, for which she is currently contributing editor. From 1992 to 1994 she was head of the Museum of Contemporary Art, Luigi Pecci in Prato. She currently lives in Rome, where she writes about contemporary art, teaches meditation and produces olive oil on her farm in Sabina.

Bibliography

Almaas, A.H.
The Void, Diamond Books, Berkley 1986
The Point of Existence, Diamond Books, Berkley 1996
The Pearl Beyond Price, Shambhala Publications, Boston 2001
Spacecruiser Inquiry, Shambhala Publications, Boston 2002
The Inner Journey Home, Shambhala Publications, Boston 2004
The Unfolding Now, Shambhala Publications, Boston 2008

Bayda, Ezra
At Home in the Muddy Water, Shambhala Publications, Boston 2003
Being Zen, Shambhala Publications, Boston 2002

Buber, Martin
The Way of Man – Ten Rungs, Citadel Press Books, New York 2006

Castaneda, Carlos
The Second Ring of Power, Simon & Schuster, New York 1977
The Power of Silence: Further Lessons of Don Juan, Simon & Schuster, New York 1984
The Wheel of Time, Simon & Schuster, New York 1998

Costantino, Avikal E.
Freedom to Be Yourself. Mastering the Inner Judge, IBI publications, Sydney 2007

Kimura, Yasuhiko Genku
Self-responsibility, Self-integrity and Freedom from the Guru, VIA Publications 2004
Creating a culture of responsibility, VIA Journal vol. I No. 2, 2003
Working for Good, video-intervista di Jeff Klein per la rivista Flow, ,www.via-visioninaction.org

Maharaj, Nisargadatta
I Am That, The Acorn Press, Durham 1992

Mahler, Margaret
The Psychological Birth of the Human Infant: Symbiosis and Individuation, Basic Books Inc., Publishers, New York 1975

Osho
The Psychology of the Esoteric, Library, www.osho.com
The Ultimate Alchemy, vol.1, Library, www.osho.com
Hari Om Tat Sat, Library, www.osho.com
Tao: The Three Treasures, Vol 3, Library, www.osho.com
Seeds of Wisdom, Library, www.osho.com
The Golden Future, Library, www.osho.com
The Inner Journey, Library, www.osho.com
The Guest, Library, www.osho.com

Tolle Eckhart
Ripples on the Surface of Being, an interview by Andrew Cohen. What is Enlightenment magazine, September-December 2006

Williamson, Marianne
Return to Love: Reflections on the Principles of 'A Course in Miracles', Harper & Collins, New York 1996

Acknowledgements

First of all, my thanks to you dear friends who have contributed to this book with your stories and your affection. Thank you for being in my life and sharing with me your authenticity, your beauty, your light and your shadow, and your vulnerability.

Thanks to you Amira, for the love and support you give me and for the space you create around me, I know that it's not always easy being around me when I'm writing, thanks for your silence and your cheerfulness.

Avikal E. Costantino
is a spiritual teacher. Curiosity, passion and love for the truth guide his teaching and are conveyed clearly and penetratingly. He is director of the Integral Being Institute which is active in Europe, Asia and Australia. He lives in Sydney.
www.integralbeing.com

BOOKS

O is a symbol of the world, of oneness and unity. In different cultures it also means the "eye," symbolizing knowledge and insight. We aim to publish books that are accessible, constructive and that challenge accepted opinion, both that of academia and the "moral majority."

Our books are available in all good English language bookstores worldwide. If you don't see the book on the shelves ask the bookstore to order it for you, quoting the ISBN number and title. Alternatively you can order online (all major online retail sites carry our titles) or contact the distributor in the relevant country, listed on the copyright page.

See our website www.o-books.net for a full list of over 500 titles, growing by 100 a year.

And tune in to myspiritradio.com for our book review radio show, hosted by June-Elleni Laine, where you can listen to the authors discussing their books.

MySpiritRadio